THIS PROMISE IS FOR YOU

Spiritual Renewal and the Charismatic Movement

David Parry, OSB

THIS PROMISE IS
FOR YOU

Spiritual Renewal and the Charismatic Movement

Darton, Longman and Todd Ltd

First published in Great Britain in 1977
by Darton, Longman and Todd Ltd
89 Lillie Road, London SW6 4SU
© 1977 David Parry OSB

ISBN 0 232 51382 1

Printed in Great Britain by
The Anchor Press Ltd and bound by
Wm. Brendon & Son Ltd, both of Tiptree, Essex

Reprinted 1978
Reprinted 1979

Contents

Foreword

Every charismatic has a story of what happened to make him so. In September 1974, I was invited to attend a prayer meeting of charismatics at the Benedictine Priory of Christ the King, Cockfosters, London. I accepted this invitation rather unwillingly, for I had other plans for that evening. It lasted two hours, and contained the phenomena I expected – praying in tongues, interpretations, singing in tongues, prophecy; someone was prayed over; others 'gave witness'; but most of it was prayer.

Altogether I was glad when it was over. Yet in spite of a reaction of dislike to some of the proceedings, and a general inability to identify with them, I took away an impression that these people were joyful, loving and addicted to prayer and that anyone who came looking for an orgy or for hysteria, would go away disappointed.

Some days later, perhaps about a week or more, I was forced to the conclusion that something had happened to me. This led to the natural questions: what and why? Still not understanding very well either the what or the why, I came to the further conclusion: 'It must be that prayer-meeting at Cockfosters!' This, although substantially correct, did not really answer the questions.

The answers I would give to these questions today are:

The Why? the total gratuitousness of God's giving.

The What? a new awareness of the nearness and of the livingness of Jesus Christ, to whom be praise and glory for ever more.

David Parry, OSB

Introduction

The idea of this book occurred to the author after he had made a retreat of seven weeks with a view to preparing himself as well as might be for the reception of that blessing referred to variously in these pages as 'the baptism of the Spirit', 'the release of the Spirit' or 'the effusion of the Spirit'. He was in no position to attend a seminar of seven weeks, and so made use of a little booklet called *Finding New Life In the Spirit* which offered him mainly scriptural texts as themes for meditations, spread out over seven weeks; he supplemented this with a book called *The Life in the Spirit Seminars* — which was addressed however not to a retreatant, but to those organising seminars for retreatants, showing them how to proceed. Against this background the author conceived the idea of writing a book to help those who, like himself, could not attend a seminar, but would be interested in receiving information on what the 'charismatic movement is about', or even for those who might want to 'pray their way' into it.

Hence the book is designed mainly for three kinds of reader: those who want a balanced presentation of what it is all about; those who positively feel the need for help of a kind they have not yet found; and beginners in the charismatic movement. It is, then, a book that may be of interest to read for some, but it is also designed as a meditation book to be used in daily stages accompanied by prayer.

The book employs the current terminology, though this is used variously by different Christian traditions. It has its difficulties. We say 'charismatic movement' but are aware that the word 'movement' suggests a human programme, activated by some kind of hierarchy, whereas we are really speaking of a movement of the Spirit of God spreading itself in a new way throughout the

1

followers of Christ. We speak of 'charisma', but are aware that this word is subject to continuous exegetical study. Likewise the term 'glossolalia', or tongue-speaking, is in general use, but there is discussion (not touched on in this work) on the exact nature of this phenomenon. The fact that most of this terminology came to life, and therefore discussion, among non-Catholic Pentecostals in North America, leaves some Catholics suspicious of it. They need not be; for they are scriptural terms, and are used in accord with Catholic doctrines.

The writing of such a book as this, intended to show that the charismatic movement does not imply the deposition or dislocation of Catholic ascetical or mystical or dogmatic teaching, involves the problem of considering the order in which to treat various matters.

Should an examination of baptism, that first conferring of the Spirit, the beginning of life in the soul, and of a flow of graces that never ceases to surround each of us, be treated first? After all, the Charismatic grace is the renewal of this, and of its increase in depth and extension. Or should the author seek to guide his reader gently into a beginning of charismatic experience, and then treat of baptism to make sure that the true picture of Christian life is presented? Either option presents some disadvantages. We have chosen the latter because we think that the normal reader (if any of us can be called normal) will want to receive the encouragement and stimulus involved in learning about or, better still, experiencing what the renewal is about first, and that this will stimulate in him a demand to enquire more closely into the gift of his baptism, and indeed other subsequent sacramental gifts. The approach then is governed by the thought. Spiritual re-animation first, doctrinal and moral consideration later. After all for many of us that corresponds to our knowledge of how the Spirit moves.

This book, as has been said, is for those who for some reason are impeded from attending prayer meetings or seminars, where they would receive instruction in this kind of experience. Some persons are already aware of a need for new animation or orientation in their lives. To all such one must say that prayer is of great importance, and they must not say 'I am a poor pray-er; so this cannot be for me.' For this could be a reason why they need the animation of this new gift of God. It is the author's hope that others may read it for information only, and others again because it pleases them to read about the graces they have already received.

Although this book was written mainly with Catholics and those of Catholic tradition in mind, it is hoped that it may be found readable also by others. For the charismatic movement is inevitably ecumenical; it is aware that God has graces, gifts and insights for all who seek to serve Him. And after all, how can a man even begin to be ecumenical, unless he believes that the Holy Spirit is at work on the other side of the fence also? For God has concern for all his children, both for their own sake, and because he loves them all.

Acknowledgement is made to *Finding New Life in the Spirit* – the Life in the Spirit Seminars; *Spiritual Gifts* by Steven Clark; *The Seven Gifts of the Holy Ghost* by Bernard Kelly; the lectures given by Father Francis Sullivan SJ at Hawkstone Park in 1975.

I would also like to express my sincere thanks to all who have helped me with this book – Father Benedict Heron OSB, without whom it would hardly have been published, Father Aldhelm Cameron-Brown OSB, Father Dewhirst IC, Brother William Harwood OSB for help with the typing and Father Cuthbert Smith for reading the proofs.

St Augustine's Abbey,
Ramsgate

Week one: Our deepest need

The world is filled with 'ordinary people'. In our daily lives we are constantly mixing with 'ordinary people'. Probably they see us in just the same light – as one more ordinary person. Yet most people have problems, and sometimes these problems lie very heavy on them. Psychiatrists rate the general level of happiness as low. Sometimes it is so low that a person is really carrying on blindly with the business of life simply because he or she has no idea of what else to do, and life presents itself as a dull or even oppressive corridor without turnings. Often at the heart of the 'ordinary person's' problems lies a spiritual problem, even *the* spiritual problem: 'What on earth am I to do with my life? How can I find the answer to my deepest need?' Even persons who sincerely practise religion may still feel this sense of emptiness, as if their religion had somehow not brought them the actual joy they needed. It has brought them, no doubt, to a greater or lesser degree, orientation as to what the purpose of life is, and how good living is to be distinguished from evil; but sometimes the prospect of joy is associated for them also with a distant hereafter. There is still a deeply felt need in the now; indeed there may be a feeling that those who are not controlled by any religious belief have a better chance of finding present joy than those whose beliefs deny them the possibility of a search without limitations.

In fact in either case the need that is being experienced is the need for salvation. This is our deepest need; once recognised it is a concept that imposes itself. But can we find and experience this thing they call salvation? Salvation, that is, from present unhappiness, emptiness, disorientation, suffering, sin, whatever extends darkness over our lives. It is at any rate worth a diligent enquiry; even (if need be) a fresh enquiry, for the matter surely warrants it.

This quest, if we set about it, will lead us to a new commitment, even if we are already committed. Hence it involves a certain openness to such a possibility, and this section is the most arduous part of the journey into the Kingdom of God. For this reason you will need to pray — or to try to pray — as much as you can during this week. Bear in mind that God's action in you is always the first thing; it is through the action of His grace or help that this sense of a need for new orientation begins to make itself felt in you. This is the start of a new development, in which God leads the way.

Day 1: The power of evil

For it is not against human enemies that we have to struggle, but against the Sovereignties and the Powers who originate the darkness in this world, the spiritual army in the heavens.

Eph 6: 12

One does not have to be a theologian to recognise man's proneness to sin; it is written large all over human history and in the world around us. The theologian refers to 'original sin', meaning this innate moral weakness, and he is much occupied with the question: How, if God made man good, do we find ourselves so inclined to evil, so unable to continue in a right path? We need not take up this question here, let us content ourselves with two points — man is a morally sick animal and God, who is good, has not made him to be like that.

Certainly man is a morally weak thing, liable under pressure to total collapse. Who has not seen it? Who has not also felt it?

And this weakness leads to the moral pollution of his environment. He lives in the kind of world in which sin is the normal climate. Sin breeds sin, and we sink hopelessly in the mire.

6

This much is a matter of common observation, but it is not the whole story. There are forces of evil at work which lead man to a deeper commitment to evil. We cannot undertake to prove this by reason; we can say that it fits all too well with observed evidences; we can say that at times men have felt a very real sense of being up against such evil.

In fact such evil forces lie behind the evil that is in us. It is a mystery, this malignity that is at times evident by deduction, occasionally palpable. It is not a case for proof, so much as a case for realisation: what has to be realised is that individual evil acts are not really to be seen as simple detached 'falls' through a weak inability to do the better thing. No, evil is more like a sea, in which drops coalesce, form a pool, a river, a flood, a torrent; or like a dark night in which, as individual lights fail, a blackness takes over all.

St Paul in the text quoted above is perfectly conscious of the 'powers of darkness' who provoke wickedness and sin, and of the connection between sin which is moral death and that death which is physical. Suffering, whether mental, moral or physical is in a way a hinterland between the happiness for which God made us and the kingdom of darkness which seeks to engulf us. It is then a partial extension of evil, sometimes the fruit of moral evil, sometimes a source of future evil; sometimes it is neither, but still a shadow falling over God's children.

We need then to be thoroughly persuaded that our battle for life and light and joy and gladness and fulfilment is ultimately a battle against sin and death and blindness and degradation, of which the powers of darkness are the ultimate organisers, profiting as they do by our inability to see clearly where salvation lies or to turn strongly to it.

But God has no intention of allowing victory over mankind to go to the evil ones. We have to understand His plans for their defeat, and for our liberation, indeed our victory.

Let us stop today simply at a deep awareness of the fact that there is something very wrong with the world (although it also contains much that is good) and that this something produces deep and widespread unhappiness — an unhappiness from which we ourselves have not escaped.

And this state of affairs is not entirely due to man; nor can it

7

be put right by man. We have to turn to God, and see, as far as we can, in what terms He provided a solution.

Let then your prayer today be one of intense desire and aspiration that whatever part of your being, be it much or little, lies under the sway of the evil one, may be liberated from this dominion; let it also be an act of faith that God has the power to do this for you. And do not forget that He is near you as you are praying, caring for you far more than you are able to perceive.

Day 2: The plans of God

Lord, has the time come? Are You going to restore the Kingdom of Israel?

Acts 1: 6

Many of us, having learnt that God is all-powerful and all-loving, expect to see His plans for the world unrolled in a successful campaign worthy of such attributes. For us this is a logical consequence, and an inevitable sequel. We are not greatly different from the disciples who, having passed from faith in Christ to despair at His crucifixion, and then back to hope again on His resurrection, asked Him simply: Lord, has the time come? Are you going to restore the Kingdom to Israel?[1] To them it was natural to suppose that now, after His manifest triumph in His resurrection, He would unfold His banners, lead forward the conquering army, establish universal peace. . . .

His reply was perfectly clear as to how things would proceed, but we may surmise it was not at that moment clear to them. He said:—

It is not for you to know times or dates, that the Father has decided by His own authority,

8

But you will receive *power when the Holy Spirit comes upon you,*
And then you will be My *witnesses* not only in Jerusalem, but
   throughout Judaea and Samaria, and indeed to the ends of
   the earth.[1]

There are three points here: they were not to expect to know
such times or dates as the Father had decided for the manifestation of the complete triumph of His Son; the complicated
historical process and its completion in total triumph would indeed take place, but He would not expound its visible progress;
secondly, they would receive power, to carry out their mission
and carry forward His Kingdom; but it would not be the kind of
power they had then in mind, but a new mysterious power of
which at that time they had little concept, though they had seen
its effectiveness in Him; this power was that of possessing the
Holy Spirit, or – expressed otherwise – the power of the Spirit
Himself working through them. Hence their life would not be
that of conquistadores, of conquerors, but of witnesses, a word
that soon came to mean 'martyr'.* Through their witness the
Spirit would express Himself with power, confirming their
'word by the signs that accompanied it'.

The Apostles would have been greatly astonished at that moment if they had known then that within a matter of weeks, they
would, in the absence of their Master, all be gaoled and receive a
full-scale flogging each by order of the Sanhedrin, the supreme
religious council of their people; and would nevertheless continue with joy to stand every day in the temple and to visit
private houses so that 'their proclamation of the good news of
Christ Jesus was never interrupted'.[2]

Yet the Apostles and the New Testament writers generally
leave the impression that, desiring Christ's return so urgently,
they retained an expectation of seeing it, even as they disclaimed
a knowledge of its date. How happy they would have been had
they had a vast vision of the successive ages in which souls, great
and small[3] would be saved and of how the Kingdom of Christ
would grow in size and variety and glory far beyond their imagination, and ours. Although they and their converts knew very

* The Greek word 'martyr' is used in the *Acts of the Apostles* mainly in the sense of
witness (1: 8) in *Revelation* it mostly corresponds to our English word 'martyr' (17: 6).

well what they were witnessing to and dying for, yet it would have added another dimension to their sense of election, if they could have known the extension through time and space that God intended to give to their witness. Even for them it seems true that the vastness of the panorama of God's plans for salvation of all men was not fully clear.

God's ways, then, are above our ways as the heavens are above the earth and His thoughts above our thoughts.[4] There is always the tension that we want an earthly solution, immediate and practical, to our earthly situations. But God's methods are different. He begins with an infusion of the Spirit, and with the infusion of the Spirit His plans begin to be comprehensible; with the increase of the infusion of the Spirit they command our total surrender, — a surrender compounded of joy, love and admiration. Nor does this mean that God does not get round to the practical problems which seem to us the primary concern. He gets round to them — but often in ways we could not foresee. He works within the heart of man. Practical results will follow, even amazing ones. Yet of the *historical scene as a whole*, it remains true that it is not for us to know the times and the dates that the Father has decided by His own authority. We walk always, then, with a mixture of faith, of power and of acceptance of what we do not understand.

But always we become more convinced that if God's ways are not our ways, they are much better ones. Better because more powerful; indeed His are the only ways that can touch the recesses of man's heart where reside the qualities of joy and peace and love. The understanding of this is an ongoing process — we are not unlike the Apostles in our expectations, and will remain so, until slowly we are taught to think otherwise.

Let us in our prayer today make a surrender of our own wisdom and ask God to infuse His own.

Day 3: The meaning of salvation

That night God appeared to Solomon and said 'Ask what you would like me to give you.' Solomon replied to God, 'Give me wisdom and knowledge to act as leader of this people. . . .

II Chron 1: 7, 10

Solomon's answer pleased God, for it was a great and a high spiritual gift that he asked for, and not material prosperity. Hence he received his request and much more, so that his reign was reckoned the high point of the prosperity of his people. And yet, as the Scripture tells, the gift was not enough; Solomon still failed in fidelity to God, and even laid the seeds from which subsequent disaster would develop.

We may conclude then that what man needs most cannot be comprised simply in the word 'wisdom'; still less in the word 'power'. Solomon had a good supply of both, and yet went wrong. What is it then that we need most of God if He says to us: 'Ask what you would like me to give you?' The answer in one word is: salvation from the evils that beset us. Salvation! What exactly does this word cover, this thing of which we have an absolute need?

It covers three things essentially: liberation from the evils that are outside us, liberation from the evils that are inside us, and the fact of belonging to the family of God. Each of these things needs to be pondered in depth.

The evils that are outside us are not difficult to recognise; indeed it is against them that we spend so much time protesting. These are all the material evils of life, those which arise from injustice, oppression, seduction (for evil does not always present itself as something nasty – quite the contrary), contention, whether at the political, social or domestic level. They comprise all the things that weigh us down, or torment or sadden us, and which we see as external evils. Few people live without some such trials in their lives; some are overwhelmed by them.

Evils from inside we often recognise, but often, also, we fail to do so. Being self-centred, we mostly measure good and evil,

11

good persons or nasty ones, by their effect on us; but the reality is far more complicated. There are evils in us, which are partly the cause of outside factors proving hostile to us. Thus we suffer from moral evils; the habits of sin, the effects of the habits of sin on our personality, the effects of turning away from good over a period of time, and the effects which this in turn has on others; or it may be that some form of oppression which in itself is an outside evil, has lit a flame of resentment and hatred within us. Nor is un-recognised resentment less powerful in its interior effects than recognised resentment; it can warp very deeply. Then, on the psychological level, who shall declare that life has left no deposit of evil within him? This can and often does take the form of hidden fears. Fears beget all sorts of things; they produce a fertile soil for misunderstandings, a sense of being ill-used (not quite the same thing as the outside oppression which we spoke of before!). Above all, fears constrict the heart, making the reception and offering of love difficult or impossible. We need then im-peratively to be delivered from such darknesses as have covered an area, great or small, of our personality.

For all these things our Lord taught us to pray in the words: Deliver us from evil. The most accurate translation of this text gives the meaning: Deliver us from the Evil One. In practice it will come to the same thing. For the kingdom of darkness has many ramifications, but they are inter-connected.

Thirdly, we need absolutely to belong; to belong, that is to the Kingdom of God. Actually we never really stand in complete isolation; we always belong, willingly or unwillingly, to a landscape, a situation, a civilization, a family. Our urgent need is to belong in the fullest sense to the Kingdom of God, in which all equally are sons and daughters, for the family of God is closely knit indeed.

When God planned the salvation of the human race, he took all these things into consideration. He knew far better than we do what gift we should need to ask for.

A good prayer for today is simply the Our Father.

Father,
Thy Kingdom come . . .
Deliver us from evil.

Day 4: Jesus is the liberator

Jesus said, 'I am the resurrection and the life — if anyone believes in Me, even if he dies, he will live; and whoever lives and believes in Me will never die. Do you believe this?'

John 11: 25, 26

Since evil is a fact in our world, and one that evinces its immense power, it was not enough for the salvation of mankind that God should reveal the difference between good living and bad; knowledge is not enough. Nor would a display of divine omnipotence have altogether met the case. God willed to save man through man; that man should throw off the coils of the evil power through man; that what had failed should prove itself a triumphant success.

This called for an extraordinary action on his part. We believe that God sent His only Son in the form of man, to walk our earth and work our redemption; human in all things except sin, strong with the strength of God, this man could and did conquer the power of evil. He did it indeed *radically*, in depth in His own person, *in extent* through all those who adhere to Him.

Thus we see that God confronted the power of evil with a yet stronger power for good. The power of darkness with a yet stronger force of light; the power of death with Himself, the source of all life, and, for man fallen into the clutches of death — the Resurrection. Battles are won by power, and it is this power of Christ that we need to grasp, to submit to, to assimilate into ourselves.

In the passage quoted above Our Lord asserts His identity with complete calm: 'I am the Resurrection and the Life.' His task, which He will achieve by the power of God, is to restore life and health and freedom and joy to every man coming into this world who will believe in Him.

So God's plan of salvation is less a matter of belief in a doctrine (though it is essential that we do believe all that Christ taught) than of faith in Christ, total submission of mind and heart to Him as Lord and Redeemer, as the 'one who was to come into this

13

world' sent by God for this very purpose. It is by this recognition first, and then by submission to Him that we come under His Lordship, and that life flows from Him to us; and so internally, but working outwards, are met and answered those needs of man, protection from evil, deliverance from his inner wounds, membership of the divine family. Clearly all this demands an act of faith in Him, that He is just this One, and can do these things. That is why time and time again a Gospel story will end with the words: 'Go in peace; your faith has made you whole.' Not the most closely reasoned argument in the world can confer this faith in the uniqueness of Christ; it is a gift of God; but it is a gift that is always offered, a gift that is not static, but, being also an attitude in the mind, one that can and does grow ever stronger by its being put into use. It is an initial vision that grows ever clearer as we become more conscious of the reality that we hold. But always it remains unearned, unmerited, a gift that is totally gratuitous, yet not a matter of speculation, for God is bound by His own promises.

Those who have practised faith all their lives will understand this; those who (whether they bear the Christian name or not) have not done so, have here to make a leap, to pay their money down as it were, and say 'Yes, Lord: Here is my submission, with all that it will entail in my life! Show me Yourself, Your Lordship, and Your love. Let me have this new life, this resurrection of which You speak; not, Lord, as an idea that my brain can conceive, but as power that penetrates my veins and my being.'

Christ then, God made man, is the unique source of salvation because He is the unique source of power. Let us adore Him as such. And bear in mind it is enough that you do your part as well as you can; He will have more things to say to you later; and perhaps not much later either.

Reading: John 11: 1-46.

Prayer: Grant, Lord, that I may experience the power of Your resurrection. Lord, grant me stronger faith.

Day 5: Why Christ suffered

As it was His purpose to bring a great many of His sons to glory, it was appropriate that God . . . should make perfect through suffering the leader who would take them to their salvation.

Heb 2: 10

We recognise in Christ the One of Power sent to work salvation for man. If we read the Gospels with attention we are struck by the compelling quality of Christ's teaching, its authority and its simplicity, its rejection of all cant, and its spontaneity; we are struck too by the loving out-going compassionate personality depicted by four different writers from their separate angles. Yet all four of them give an apparently disproportionate amount of space to their account of Christ's death. (How much space, proportionately, do other writers devote to the death of the hero?) Yet this is not because the subject was a pleasant one; it was a most ignominious, cruel, public execution, in itself a most painful subject. The amount of space devoted to it then is due, not to its being a pleasant subject, but to its importance. Of all the important things Christ did the most important was to die.

But why? Many 'fruits' of Christ's death may be listed, and should be listed and pondered. Let us take the words of the *Letter to the Hebrews* for the central theme[1]; 'As it was His purpose to bring many of His sons into glory, it was appropriate that God, for whom everything exists, and through whom everything exists, should make perfect through suffering, the leader who would take them to their salvation. For the one who sanctifies, and the ones who are sanctified, are of the same stock. . . .'

Christ was fulfilling a cosmic law in the sense that, becoming identified with us, He accepted liability with us for our sins; indeed, being our leader (was He not the Chosen, the one sent by God?), He accepted the whole liability. The Cross proclaims simultaneously: Death is the penalty of sin, and love unto death is the quality of the Redeemer. And love unto death, even for a pack of sinners, was the stronger of the two. Do we not recognise that he who risks his life for another holds that other dearer than

15

his life? Loves him more than his life? But God-made-man did not merely undergo a risk; He delivered Himself up freely that death might claim all that death can claim, and the payment of sin be paid to the total extent conceivable – and so came out victorious, saying 'See, I have more love for you yet. It is inexhaustible!' Before such a love all sin is impotent, all hatred inefficacious, all evil powerless. Henceforth He is victor on behalf of the human race over all the ills that can beset it. And what is love about but sharing? His victory is for sharing with us:

'Since all the children share the same blood and flesh, he too shared equally in it, so that by his death he could take away all the power of the devil, who had power over death, and *set free* all those who had been held in slavery all their lives by fear of death.[2]

'It is not easy to die even for a good man – though of course for someone really worthy, a man might be prepared to die – but what proves that God loves us is that Christ died for us while we were sinners.'[3]

So his mission cost Him a good deal. He did not achieve His power to free all except at His own cost. And it was of the essence of the matter that He was one of us, capable of suffering just as we do, but towering above us in His consuming love for the liberation of each of us. We have but to adhere to Him to come into the realm of His liberating power. We do not achieve our salvation; we accept it from Him who has already achieved it. We have but to enter in.

Yet, we must note, we have to enter into the whole of it. We cannot say: Lord give me the fruits, but please cover up with a veil the suffering and ignominy by which You attained them. For the Cross has to be accepted if the Resurrection is to be shared. For it was on the Cross that He won us, won the victory on our behalf, and it was in the Resurrection that His victory was proclaimed by God. If you want to take part in the victory procession, do not seek to hide during the battle. They are one. And we have nothing to fear. For if in our life we imitate Him in the one, the arduous gaining of the victory, we do so by the power of the other, the infusion of the Spirit of the victorious Christ, that He sends so liberally into our hearts. He is victor. He wants to reap the fruits of His victory. You are the fruits.

If you want a little prayer for today, say with the centurion who stood below the Cross of Christ in the hour of greatest gloom. 'In truth this man was a Son of God.'[3] Truly He was the Son of God.[4]

Day 6: We learn from His suffering

It was essential that He should in this way become completely like His brothers, so that He should be a compassionate and trustworthy high priest, able to atone for human sins.

Heb 2: 17

It is a cosmic law, and one we recognise in our own affairs, that where offence has been given some kind of atonement, repentance or apology is called for before the matter can be laid to rest. Even if we leave out all question of punishment due, or measure of retribution, it remains that an offender must make at least some gesture of recognition of his offence and of his need for pardon before the disturbance of right order can be considered repaired. Without such a gesture of reparation life in the household goes on, but it is not the same; the ghost of the ill that was done, of the offence that was given, somehow lives on, and the breach in unity is unhealed. Seen in this light, Christ the chosen one, the head of the human race, would have needed to make an act of reparation to the Father on our behalf – but that would still be a long way from His terrible death on the Cross. Why was such a death necessary? To satisfy the demands of a wrathful Father? Certainly not. Why then?

We should often consider the mystery of the Cross, not to sentimentalise over Christ's sufferings, for He suffers no more, but to draw the lessons which this His supreme saving act should teach us.

1. Isaiah wrote: 'Ours were the sufferings He bore, ours the sorrows He carried. He was pierced through for our faults, crushed for our sins. On Him lies the punishment that brings us peace, and through His wounds we are healed. We had all gone astray like sheep, each taking his own way, and the Lord burdened Him with the sins of all of us.'[1]

It was, then, the divine plan, fully accepted by Our Blessed Lord, that He should carry the fulness of the burden of guilt that belongs to each of us, and to all of us. That each of us should be able to see and to say: 'Yes, He has carried the punishment of my sins; I see it and bow down my head, ashamed that anyone could love me so much, yet accepting the 'peace' with God that He has won for me with joy, and knowing that here in this passion lies the power through which 'we are healed'. His wounds, our healing; therein lies the secret of his power.

2. The Crucifixion was the awful drama in which the powers of evil were allowed to do their worst, and to manifest themselves in all their ugliness. In this drama these powers are overcome by our wondrous humanity, for with this Man they prevail not at all. Physically they kill Him, but His spirit defies them, not in pride, but in obedience and love.

3. For this clash with evil was also simultaneously the most convincing demonstration of divine love. Christ was to manifest the love of the Father. He manifested it, in a way we understand, as man. He said: 'Greater love than this no man has than to lay down his life for his friends.'[2] This is the ultimate test and He fulfilled it to the letter. Pause for a moment and count up the number of persons for whom you are sure that you would readily die. How many of these belong to your intimate family circle, resting on a human bond? How many lie outside it? Know for sure that you lie inside the circle of those for whom Christ's love prompted Him to surrender His life to a most ignominious death. Are you not then one of a very 'intimate circle' of His friends for whom He was prepared to fulfil to the letter the ultimate witness of love?

4. Moreover it seems that in this stark agony, He was to learn experimentally the meaning of all the sufferings, however

brought about, of the rest of us. He was brought low, to our lowest level, which is ultimately that of death, that He, although sent of God, might share our lot in all things. This is the significance of the text already cited; it was essential that He should in this way become completely like His brothers, so that He could be a compassionate and trustworthy high priest of God's religion, able to atone for human beings. To be 'compassionate' is really to 'suffer with' another, and by His passion and death Christ descended into our areas of suffering and death. God willed that He should win His power in this way, that we might have the more confidence in Him, but it is essential that we see this as the way by which God led Him, in obedience [3] in order to confer supreme power on Him.

5. It is essential to see this, because fundamentally we win similar victories by virtue of the same power. Later there will be talk of charismatic gifts and of signs of the divine authority and of the joyful life in the Spirit. But we must not dissociate ourselves from Christ who makes of us witnesses to Himself, passing on the same message, sharing in the same redeeming work, in His own language 'carrying our cross after Him' but always now in the power of the Spirit that He will send us.

Prayer: Teach me, Lord, to understand better the meaning of Thy suffering and death.

Day 7: Christ invites us to His Kingdom

He has taken us out of the power of darkness, and created a place for us in the Kingdom of the Son that He loves, and in Him we gain our freedom, the forgiveness of our sins.

Col 1: 13-14

We have considered Christ's victorious battle on the Cross, a battle fought solely on our account. Now let us think of the results,

19

the spoils of victory. Firstly, God takes us 'out of the power of darkness', for that power is essentially defeated now, and gives us 'a place in the Kingdom of the Son that He loves'. For how could He refuse or do otherwise in the face of the plea of His Son? Not that the Father loves us less than the Son, but it is His pleasure that we be received into His Son's Kingdom by virtue of His Son's pleading for us. 'And in Him we gain freedom; we shall be delivered from our sins, our bitternesses, hatreds, interior corruptions, whatever be the forms of sin that plague us, for perhaps they are many. With this freedom from sin are lifted the sad consequences of sin that surround us all our lives.

As we end this week we need to be very clear about three things:

There is a 'power of darkness', very real, comprising all that betrays our happiness; the exact borderline to which this power extends is not clearly defined but it pervades human living; by ourselves we do not escape from it. But let us firmly resolve to do so by the power of Christ.

Secondly there is the 'Kingdom of the Son that He loves' – which is the exact opposite of the other. In this Kingdom love overcomes hate, humility overcomes pride, chastity overcomes sexual slavery, joy overcomes sorrow, healing overcomes sickness, life overcomes death.

Thirdly, the entry to this Kingdom of His Son is through the forgiveness of sins, which we must seek anew. And on the other side of the gate of this Kingdom lies true human freedom.

Yes, there is a condition, a very real one. We have to turn to Jesus, 'the author of our salvation' with all the sincerity of which we are capable. We may not feel capable of any very fine sentiments, or indeed capable of answering for our future improvement. That is not the immediate question, which is simply: Do you want, do you accept with all your heart this salvation that is offered you? In that heart of hearts of yours, known to you alone, where no man enters, do you accept that this Man loved you unto death, as no one else has ever loved you? and that, loving you so, He desires to go further to heap up in you the fruits, the enrichment, that He has the power to confer on you? Do you want this? Yes, it will mean quite a change in the person you really are. You will not have to achieve this change – indeed you cannot do so. What you have to do is to accept, and accepting, surrender. You have to make a discovery: that since Jesus loves you to the point of death, and is still loving you in just the same way, there is a response in your heart, which says simply: 'Lord, I love You. Lord, I do not understand how You come to love me so, but I accept that it is so, and, accepting, I wish to make some return. The only return I can make lies in my heart. What else does one offer a lover but one's heart? So, Lord, I turn to You; work in me that change that will enable me to make a return to You.'

For your prayer today, recall the intense way in which Christ has sought out your soul, and say to Him: 'Lord, work in me, so that I may make to You some return of love. Leave me not like the barren fig tree,[1] but since You desire my love, and I am so helpless in the matter, put love in my heart that I may give it back to You. Amen Lord Jesus.

Here is a prayer from the psalms on the same theme:

Keep me from the way of error
and teach me your law.
I have chosen the way of truth
With your decrees before me
I bind myself to do your will
Lord do not disappoint me.
I will run the way of your commands;
You give *freedom* to my heart.

                                        Ps 118: 25-32

Week two: Turning to God through Christ

In the meditations of last week, we saw that our deepest need was for salvation, that salvation which comes from God, through the sending of His son Jesus Christ. It follows that the next step is to turn to Him and ask for this with confidence.

For some who have not served God with their lives this may seem very difficult. They know that they are disorientated, or simply without orientation; and with perplexity and fumbling they find themselves being drawn, not always by logic, but by sheer need to address the great God in whom they have not really believed, and who at best seems a hazy, semi-reality to them. A turning is called for, a leap that calls for a new kind of courage. God is very near – although they think that they are very far from Him.

Not all, by any means, become conscious of the call in this way. There are many who already serve God, lead a regular Christian life and follow the commandments, but have a sense of not really having found the Lord Himself; they are not particularly joyful; they do not think much of Christian power, for it is hardly a reality to them; the wonderful promises of the Gospel seem meant for other times and other people – in a word, they are unfulfilled. These too need to turn to Christ, to experience Him directly, and to rejoice in His loving presence, and glory in His power.

There are other sorts and conditions of men who feel this need and are invited by this very feeling to take a step forward. Some Christians indeed want to serve the Lord in simplicity and love, but are held back by enslavement to some evil habit. They know their habit is wrong, but are trapped, and have to learn that the Lord Jesus can and will set them free. Their business, the contribution to their own salvation which they have to make here and now, is to turn to Him.

Or again there are those who have been scarred by their past, and walk around wounded persons, knowing no remedy for their kind of hurt. For them no less, the healer is Christ. They must turn to Him.

The pages that follow this week are designed specifically to help the reader to make this kind of approach to Jesus.

Day 1: Bartimaeus, who appealed to Christ

As He left Jericho with His disciples and a large crowd, Bartimaeus (that is the son of Timaeus), a blind beggar, was sitting at the side of the road. When he heard that it was Jesus of Nazareth, he began to shout and to say: 'Son of David, Jesus, have pity on me'. And many of them scolded him, and told him to keep quiet, but he only shouted all the louder, 'Son of David, have pity on me.' Jesus stopped and said, 'Call him here.' So they called the blind man. 'Courage,' they said, 'get up; He is calling you.' So throwing off his cloak, he jumped up, and went to Jesus. Then Jesus spoke, 'What do you want Me to do for you?' 'Rabbuni,' the blind man said, 'Master, let me see again.' Jesus said to him, 'Go, your faith has saved you.' And immediately his sight returned and he followed Him along the road'

Mark 10: 46-52[1]

Bartimaeus was of no interest to anybody. He had nowhere to go, nothing to do, nothing to offer; he sat useless by the wayside. He was a beggar and there was nothing to be had from him; he could not even keep himself; he was blind and could not even enjoy the free gift of God's landscape, or the sight of human beauty or man's works. He could, however, hear a confused noise in the distance – a crowd evidently coming nearer.

'What is that about?'

24

'Jesus of Nazareth, a wonderworker, a prophet.'
'Son of David, Jesus, have pity on me!'
'Be quiet; you're interrupting his teaching!'
'SON OF DAVID, HAVE MERCY ON ME!!!'
And Jesus is touched with compassion. 'Call him to me,' He says; and then, 'What can I do for you?' 'My sight . . . to see again.' And so the request is granted.

We must realise that Jesus worked this wonder purely out of compassion and love for Bartimaeus — not that He might add His name to a list of persons cured, miracles achieved or persons converted. His motive was personal compassion.

Here you have to identify with Bartimaeus: to realise that yours is an essential poverty; the more true this seems to you, the less reason you have for thinking that you are alone: on the contrary here is the One whose preoccupation is with such. The more you identify with Bartimaeus, the more you will understand that, as Christ advances down the road, the closer comes to you the reality of love. He loves you personally, as He loved Bartimaeus. Hold hard on to that; as far as you can, ask for your liberation; that like Bartimaeus you may throw off your cloak, jump up, struggle towards Him, for He is calling for you. This is the individual personal wonder repeated in all times and everywhere — that the Master is calling for us; and this simply because He loves us.

Remain then a while considering this fact: Christ is coming your way. It may be, that if you have always been among His servants, that He was always 'coming your way'; but this thought should not put you off. For love is always coming, always calling, until it achieves its desire.

The gift of sight that Bartimaeus received came exclusively from the compassion of Christ, and in that compassion He manifested God's love. Bartimaeus did nothing to earn the miracle; there was nothing he could do. It was a total gift. This will always be our position with God. We can accept His freely offered gifts or we can refuse them; we can respond, but properly speaking we cannot earn. This thought is reassuring, for it throws us immediately on to the loving mercy of God. And that is what we have somehow to come to realise — that this loving mercy is extended to us freely, fully and invitingly, simply because God is superabundantly good. Every act of faith, or would-be faith, in that goodness is a step on the right road. When we can say that we know that God is good because we have found it so ourselves, then indeed we shall not need urging to seek more of this goodness.

For our prayer today, let us say with Bartimaeus, 'Jesus, Son of David, have pity on me!' Let us repeat it. We do not actually need to shout, for He hears us, but we need to do our part of repeating it with entreaty. It is essential that we become convinced that God loves us, warmly, personally, effectively. He sent His Son to demonstrate this, and to convince us of it.

Day 2: The path to be followed

For God so loved the world that He gave His only son that whoever believes in Him should not perish, but have eternal life.

John 3: 16

The text which we pondered yesterday ended with the words: 'He followed Him along the road.' Let us make these words our own to the extent of asking ourselves: What shall we hear if we do follow Him along the road? What, in brief, is the sum of the message that Bartimaeus joined the throng in order to hear?

We cannot expect to penetrate this message all at once, nor to be penetrated by it all at once, but it may help to set out a conspectus, to chart the journey ahead. There are four key statements, all of which need to be understood; but bear always in mind that a fuller penetration comes with time. This is a general truth for all learners; we grasp enough to pass on, and find, after we have passed on, that what we learnt before is clearer and our grasp of it is firmer.

1. God loves you, with all the consequences that true love en-

tails; that is to say, He wants you to know the fullness and happiness of which your nature is capable, in this life and hereafter.

2. Man is sinful and separated by his sins from God. That is why the last statement is so often meaningless to him. He has other ambitions, expectations, desires; he does not believe that God is the answer to anything. Maybe he has faith enough to believe that God exists and has His rights; that it will work out badly if he trespasses on God's preserves. 'Man's sinfulness' is a very comprehensive phrase; it includes those who seek to wipe out His name, those who are content to live immorally in known wickedness, those who live respectably but without reference to God, etc. And it includes to a certain extent many Christians who are not living 'in a state of sin', but yet are separated from Him by the fact that they are not consciously motivated by His love. Tradition, the sense of duty, the need for a coherent attitude to life, Christian education, all play their part in the life of a person who by no means rejects God's love, but somehow remains untouched by it. Alas! This man still belongs, psychologically at least, among those who are of this world in their preoccupations, outlook and values. He is not drawing nearer to God in any way, other than by the daily approach of his death. If somewhere in this category we find ourselves, then the statement that God loves us will sound but faintly in our ears.

3. The only person who can transfer us out of this spiritually lifeless category is Jesus Christ, Our Lord. Only He has the power to make this internal change in us. Only He can grant us to know the reality of God's love. And who in terms of ordinary human relationships does not want to be loved? Loved, that is, not as the object of some improvement but just as he is, with the kind of love that makes him feel good, and which causes love to blossom in his heart in return. Let us not then be disheartened if, through neglect or ignorance or even in spite of long years of service, we feel a long way off from God, and lack the inner energy or dynamism to do anything serious about it.

Yet we have to do just one thing; to attempt to grasp that Christ is the one source of inner change. 'God so loved the world that He gave His only Son that whoever believes in Him should not perish, but have eternal life. That is why Christ loved Bartimaeus; he was fulfilling this mission, manifesting the love of the

Father which was in Himself, and with which He loved Bartimaeus. And so, not less, He loves you.

4. The fourth proposition that charts the nature of our journey is that, having sought to grasp the love of God for you, you turn to Him and accept it – just that – and accept Jesus Christ, His only Son as your Lord and Saviour and Healer, to whom you will dedicate your life. To enable you to do this He sends the Holy Spirit, who gives power to live this new life. Do not, then, be afraid and say 'I cannot do this – I am not that kind of person – I can only live in my way – I am too old or too fixed.' For it is true that you cannot do anything spiritual by yourself; there is nothing wrong in recognising this. It is as far as it goes perfectly true. But it does not go far enough. The heart of the matter is that you must turn to God as well as you can, and He, out of His infinite goodness, supplies the strength, a strength accompanied by joy. For anything else would not represent Him as He really is.

Turn then to Him and pray, however briefly, that He may touch you with His love, and activate your response.

Day 3: Divine providence

They have not understood that I was the one looking after them,
I led them with reins of kindness,
With leading strings of love.
I was like someone who lifts an infant close against his cheek,
Stooping down to him I gave him his food.

Hos 11: 3-4

The truth that God loves human beings tenderly was not first revealed by Christ. The Old Testament is full of it; full too of complaints by God that His advances are not being reciprocated.

28

The prophecy of Hosea from which the above lines come shows an alternation of the tenderness of invitation to love God, with threats of the evils which befall when God, repulsed, withdraws His hand. In the Old Testament the nature of God's love is revealed progressively and more and more clearly; also that it is a love not merely for a single race, even if the Jewish race was chosen for special favours, but of the whole human race. Nor are wicked persons excluded from God's concern. Thus the book of Jonah, which shows God's mercy to the Assyrian city of Nineveh (which dominated the ancient world somewhat as the Nazi Reich briefly dominated a large part of our own), ends with the words: 'And am I not to feel sorry for Nineveh, the great city, in which there are more than a hundred and twenty thousand persons, to say nothing of all the animals?' In these words was shown also that God loved not men only, but all His creation, animals and all living things; the sparrows who fall to the ground.

So before Christ the fact that God loved the human race and continued to do so, in spite of its sins, had been revealed through the prophets. God did indeed draw souls to Himself in those days; the books of Ruth, Tobias, etc. give us pictures of devout worshippers of God in all their simplicity. But it was not in itself a fully effective revelation; it was not enough; it was but a preparation. Man needed to be able to see God's love in a form that was immediately recognisable. So He sent His own Son to manifest the quality of His love. In His Son, He stooped down to walk on this earth; in His Son He lifted up all humanity to hold Him as 'an infant close against his cheek'. We have then to see in Christ — His words, His teaching, His reactions to human situations, His passion and death — God's manifestation of love, the fulfilment of the promises of the Old Testament. For God's promises are irrevocable; if man in His perversity defeats them in one way, they are found fulfilled in another.

Let us pause here to observe that for some 'God sent His own Son' will be an expression of the Christian faith in which they do not believe; a fairy tale. For others, who do indeed believe, it will evoke no particular emotions: theirs is a tired Christianity; they have heard its doctrines all their lives, and have lived with a passive acceptance, without resistance, but also without enthusiasm. What then is at issue in these pages is that the reader

29

should discover anew the reality of the power and love of God, manifested in Jesus. Then he will know that Jesus is not just one among other men, but truly the Son of God. This was what Mark intended to convey when at the end of a stark account of Christ's passion and crucifixion, he records the words of the centurion as he looked at the dead Jesus, and said: 'Indeed this man was a Son of God!'[1] It was fundamentally an act of faith made at the bleakest of all moments. We are intended to repeat — only with a fuller, more understanding faith — these words of the centurion.

God's plans of love, then, as first manifested in the Old Testament are fulfilled in the New. They are ever being fulfilled both in ways that we understand and in ways that we shall only understand later. What we do know with absolute clearness is that God invites us, each and all, to benefit by His promises. 'They will all know me, the least, not less than the greatest, — it is the Lord who speaks — since I will forgive their iniquity and never call their sin to mind.'[2] 'To know' is to be filled with joy, and the barrier to this knowing is the 'iniquity' which pervades our whole make-up and makes that cleanness of heart by which we see God such a distant prospect. The solution is that God 'forgives' the iniquity, not merely in the negative sense of not holding it against us any more, but in the divine sense, which implies that when the obstacle is removed, divine love rushes in, taking possession, giving joy and inviting to further transformation. This is true for the least as well as for the greatest; for blind Bartimaeus as well as for Nicodemus, for the beggar at the temple entrance called the Beautiful Gate[3] no less than for 'Your Excellency, Theophilus.'

We need to understand absolutely that there lies before us this offer — and it is always a new offer — of God's love, of a love which will not be satisfied unless it makes us alive through the Spirit of Christ dwelling in our hearts. The offer is universal; equally it is personal.

Day 4: God's constancy to His promises

I myself will pasture my sheep, I myself will show them where to rest — it is the Lord God who speaks. I shall look for the lost one, bring back the stray, bandage the wounded and make the weak strong. I shall watch over the healthy and the strong. I shall be a true shepherd to them.

Ezek 34: 14-16

In the above passage notice first of all how, through the mouth of His prophet, almighty God commits Himself personally. 'I myself' he says 'will pasture', and then, for more emphasis. 'It is the Lord God who speaks': meaning that these are not the words of priest or writer or even of the prophet. No, 'they are My words, My promises, My commitment,' says God Himself.

And to whom does he commit Himself? Specifically to the lost, the erring, the hurt and wounded, and the weak and helpless. All those whose sole claim is their poverty, their plight, their necessity. For He is a compassionate God. Nor does He exclude 'the healthy and the strong' for they have received their health, their strength, their richness of personality from Him, and have a strong clear chord of praise to sing to His glory. For He is the universal shepherd.

If then God so commits Himself personally to all of us, and to each of us, whatever our shape or size, beauty or disfigurement, youth or age, have we not a duty to respond with a corresponding commitment to Him? This is what you are being called to.

In the fullness of time, Our Lord manifested in His own person what the invisible God had said of Himself by the mouth of His prophet. 'I' He said 'am the Good Shepherd; the Good Shepherd is one who lays down his life for his sheep.' This is Our Lord's favourite description of Himself, which occurs throughout the Gospels. For it was the shepherd's task to live with the sheep at all times, to know them individually, to guard them from harm — and not least to go in search of the stray ones. This task of going in search of the stray, of reclamation, Our Lord must have described and referred to on many occasions. In St Luke's Gospel

31

three parables are collected together, all with the same theme. First, the prodigal son: who could repent and walk home to an astonishingly warm welcome – to a Father already scanning the highway for his return. Second, the lost sheep: helpless no doubt, caught in brambles in all probability, but still able to bleat to draw attention to itself. Third, the lost drachma, which has rolled away and got lost under some furniture; and can do nothing at all, until at last the diligence of the housewife retrieves it.

In all these stories God is telling us either through the mouth of His prophet or even more appealingly through the mouth of His only Son that He wants us back; that we are too far off; that He is in search of us; that it is most personal. Bring home to yourself, then, as you ponder these texts, that God is telling you that He loves you, and inviting a response. The invitation is warm, tender, loving. Let your response be as much like it as you can make it. That is what He is asking for.

Read and think about the parables in *Luke* 15. They are offered as our Lord's explanation, His defence of Himself even, because He welcomes sinners and eats with them.

Day 5: Living water

If only you knew what God is offering, and who it is that is saying to you 'Give me a drink,' you would have been the one to ask, and he would have given you living water.

John 4: 10

The way had been long; our Lord had talked a lot; he sat now by Jacob's well in Samaria, tired and hungry and thirsty. For food, the disciples had gone to buy something in a neighbouring town. For drink, Jesus asked a Samaritan woman coming with her bucket to draw water. She was surprised that a Jewish religious teacher should lower himself to talk to her, should in fact cross the line of a permanent and recognised hostility to demand a small favour of a Samaritan. She was not a bad sort in spite of her lamentable matrimonial record of six husbands; but as far as she knew, this damning aspect of her life story was unknown to the Jewish religious teacher. Otherwise surely, he would not . . .

She could not have been more mistaken. He did know; and it made no difference; Samaritan or Jew, good record or bad record, his offer went out just the same. 'If only you knew who I am, and what I have to offer you.' This offering, which he describes as 'water . . . welling up to eternal life,' is the matter on which we have to dwell.

You are a thirsty traveller on life's road. You are in some way dry. It may be that you have occupied yourself with much business, filling life with one enterprise after another, or you may have thought that having a good time corresponded to the good and fulfilled life. Somehow it has not proved so. Contrariwise you may be a devout nun, monk or priest, who foreswore much that you might devote your life to the service of God. You have set out with a high intention and a confidence that He would not fail you — and you were right about that — only now is the time to let Him fulfil the promises you have rightly understood Him to make. However you come by your thirst, now is the time to turn to Him and allow Him with an open heart to give you to drink, and teach you the nature of true fulfilment. If you feel quite helpless, do this nevertheless, for this is the moment of grace for you.

Even if we have been fortunate and lived a successful life and known the joy of a deep and returned human love, we shall know that all life is a dry and dusty journey, an arid journey without the refreshment of the water of love. Indeed we shall perish of dehydration without it. All success and achievement, all gains find their meaning from the fact that they are enjoyed in the communion of love. Some are happy enough to know this from their experience. Too many know it by the opposite experience; that all the good things which may have come to them have not been adequate for their central need, which is love. Harder still is the case of those who do not feel that they have had anything positive or good, or a fair share of life's good, as they consider what life has dealt out to them. There is a kind of madness or deep down resentment which cries out: 'Since love has not come to me, I hate you all! I will take it out of you, that I may not be a complete loser in life's stakes.'

Many know that life has gone wrong for them but cannot say exactly why. And even if they know that what has gone wrong is the lack of the experience of love, they have no idea of what can be done about it. For to perceive with one's intelligence that one is a beggar is not a big step towards feeling that one has become rich.

Since this is the case of all of us to some degree, including those who are blessed with true human love (for these will be in a position to understand most easily what love is about), we need to turn to this One who offers us the living waters of His love, the real answer to our thirst. Yes! we have to feel it, to let it gurgle in our throat, to know refreshment – not merely to talk about it – but this experience will come. For the moment it is enough that you decide to turn to Him who offers you, even as He did the Samaritan woman, this living water. He made it quite clear that it was for all. On the last and greatest day of the festival (when the crowds would have been at their greatest) Jesus stood there, calling out to anyone who would listen.

> If any man is thirsty, let him come to Me!
> Let the man come and drink, who believes in Me.[1]

He was fulfilling the prophets. Isaiah wrote:

> Oh! come to the water all you that are thirsty:
> Though you have no money, come!
> ... Pay attention, come to Me
> Listen and your soul will live.[2]

There is a thirst within us, and it proclaims our need and our dependence; we have to turn to Him, accept Him on His terms, and when He gives us to drink, we shall know what He means by 'living water' now. Our immediate need is to recognise how to satisfy our deepest thirst, and to turn to Him who has the water that gives life.

34

Day 6: The nature of God's plans for us

I know the plans I have for you — it is the Lord who speaks — plans for peace, not disaster, reserving a future full of hope for you. When you call to Me, and come and pray to Me, I will listen to you. When you seek Me, you shall find Me.

Jer 29: 11-13

How many of us have any real confidence in the plans God may be making for us? Perhaps not too much. We are more interested in our own. We may react with boredom or distrust to such information as we have of the nature of God's service or of what pleases Him. Boredom; do you go to Church when you want a real live experience? or do you go with a sense of dutiful acceptance of the necessary tax to be paid for remaining on terms with God? Distrust: so often when people speak to us of accepting the will of God, they mean that we should bow our heads to the inevitable, the unpleasant — even the intolerable. This results in our associating His plans with nasty medicine. It is often our own fault that we do so, since too rarely do we stop to consider all the good things that have flowed to us from His hands. We take them all for granted.

Another reaction to the notion of God's plan is the idea that the good part of it, or at any rate the only part of it you can really trust to be good, is in the next life.

Shown in these terms talk of God's plans for us will not fall on eager ears. There is a gap between the prophet's way of speaking (and remember he speaks in the person of God) and our own understanding. He speaks of 'plans of peace', a 'future full of hope' of his attentive listening to our prayers. (And perhaps we think in our hearts, 'Well, I've tried praying').

Firstly and absolutely, lastly and finally, we must understand that the great good — the invariable and permanent good, the profoundest element in the plans of peace — which God has to communicate is His love. And let us not be ambiguous about this. Lovers have to understand one another; love has to be a joy-bringing experience, a completion, a fulfilment; and it has to fit

35

my little measure. Love is an experience both given and received, gentle or violent, smooth or tempestuous; but always an experience.

Yes, that is what God is talking about. And He talks to you. At this stage, it is enough that you stay with Him in the silence of your heart, or if that seems too remote a proposition, then just allow Him a space of time, say fifteen minutes, more if you can, in which you say:

Lord, I hear; grant me Your promises.
I understand that they are addressed to me personally.
Lord, I turn to You; I hear, I listen and I believe.
I believe not only that You are the God of theology,
but the God who made these wonderful promises that
You would lead me in the ways of your love.
I ask You to lead me in this way, knowing that You are far
more anxious to bring me joy than I am to turn to You.

We may have quite a struggle getting used to the idea that God's plans for us are the plans of a lover for the happiness and the enrichment and the joy of the one He loves.

And that this concerns the now.

For good people (meaning those who have lived religiously) the difficulty may well be that they have always confused God's plans for them with their plans for Him, or at least with the plans that He was expected by them to make, and they have not found adequate joy in the result.

For those in whose lives God has played little part, the idea that He may become an overpowering and joyful reality may seem remote. If material things have not brought much joy, is not this invisible God a still more unlikely prospect?

Whoever you are, now is the moment to turn to Him, and tell Him that you want to respond to His promises.

Day 7: The nearness of God to us

The Lord is near to all who call upon Him, to all who call upon Him in truth.

Ps 145: 18 (RSV)

For some this thought is easy to realise, for others more difficult. It is as well, in the first place, to realise that it is not a question of the extent of our imagination. A poet may write a beautiful line of poetry:

Is not my gloom after all
Shade of His hand outstretched caressingly?

And this poetry may contain truth, consoling truth too. But here and now we are not talking in metaphors or asking for an exercise of the imagination, but for a realistic attitude. It comprises two points.

1. God says He is present when we call on. Him.
2. God keeps His promises.

How do you know that He is present? Firstly, the mere fact that you are following this path, that you are performing this exercise with all the good will you are capable of is in itself evidence of His having laid His finger on you, of His calling you. There is no danger of His not 'being near'; the danger is that you take yourself away, remove yourself from the range of His voice. He may not let you, for He is a loving God and there is nowhere for you to go; but nevertheless this is a danger you should be aware of, and it is not caused by Him.

Observe that He is near to all who cry to Him. That includes you. It is important for you to grasp this personalness of His response. Wide as the world may be, countless as its population may be, He is present to you, with you, personally, in your hour of need, and of summoning. This word 'summoning' may seem a strong one, but God is bound by His promises and by His infinite goodness. The smallest and least worthy of His creatures exercises a pull over Him in its need. And much more so those who have

37

already received adoption through baptism. Know then with complete surety that God is near to you now; He is working within you, and you have to yield to Him as well as to cry to Him.

How and in what way the path is traced out by which you draw nearer to Him will be examined in subsequent weeks. It is enough now if, having pondered these declarations of His love and His personal concern for you during this past week, you rest now in as simple and deep a response as you can. Say something like this: Lord, You have declared Your love and concern for me. You have drawn near and touched me. Give me now strength and grace to turn to You, to respond to Your touch. Lord, I make an act of faith in Your Love for me, and in the reality of Your promises. Lord, lead me on.

In this, as in all else, our Lord confirms and clarifies the will of his Father. These are His instructions:[7]

> Go to your private room and when you have shut the door, pray to your Father *who is in that secret place*, and your Father who sees all that is done in secret will reward you.

This does not mean that you should not pray with companions if any are available. For Our Lord attached his own special promise to such prayer too, and it in no way contradicts these instructions (*Matt* 6: 6). The point is that our prayer should be authentic, personal, without ostentation. This also is our Lord's promise:

> Where two or three meet in my name, I shall be there with them.[2]

Nor should we lose heart if we feel that our prayer has no strength or grip, and that there is nothing much we can do about it. For our loving God knows very well of what stuff we are made, and if He extends His invitation, He extends also His power to draw us out of the pit of our incapacity and sinfulness. It is written:

> In all His promises the Lord keeps faith,

38

He is unchanging in all His works;
The Lord holds up those who stumble.
And straightens backs which are bent.

Ps 145: 14

These words are not merely a statement about God; they are the psalmist's confession of faith; they are his praise of God, and therefore a prayer. You may find much in this beautiful psalm which offers food for thought (Is God really so?), and much that is the prayer of praise. With this prayer of praise join yourself as well as you can.

Week three: Newness of life

For some people such expressions as 'the New Life' or 'Charismatic Renewal' are the cause of an immediate reaction of suspicion, even of disapproval. Is not the Church as they have always known her fully endowed already with every divine gift? Are there not seven Sacraments through which Christians receive every necessary grace? If we talk of 'New Life' is there not an inference that life was lacking before? Moreover, these charismatics seem, perhaps, to bear a resemblance to the revivalist groups which have punctuated the history of Christianity with outbursts that were both frenzied and temporary. Surely true Christianity has no need of emotional outbursts, which seem to do good as they increase fervour, but leave a sense of failure behind them as they wane?

If then we want to talk of this 'Newness of Life', we must explain that there is no suggestion of a new type of Christianity, nor of a pressure group with ideas of its own to be foisted on the whole body of the Church, or worse still, to live as an enclave on the margin of the Church.

Most of us with even a modest knowledge of church history are aware that the life of the Church can wax and wane like other human phenomena. There is nothing contradictory to our concept of faith when we read in our history books that the Church has fallen into a low state at a given time, in a given place in its history. We accept this fact, with sorrow indeed, but as a reality, even as we rejoice when, turning the page, we see that God raises up some heroic figure, filled with His Spirit, and armed with exceptional powers, to bring back a whole district or region or country to a more fervent practice of its faith. How profound an effect in enlivening the faith of thousands had such charismatic figures as St Francis of Assisi, St Vincent de Paul, St John Regis or St Peter Canisius. In each case they brought a certain new vision and spiritual renewal to those with whom they came into contact.

In our own day the Church has a more than normally hard task. Modern man is enamoured of his own scientific advances. He belittles the concept of the supernatural, and is indifferent to God's rights over him, or his love for him; and yet in another aspect he is tormented by spiritual disorientation, barrenness, hopelessness and anxiety; moreover the tide of sheer evil seems to grow remorselessly. And in the face of these challenges, who shall doubt that the Church needs all the power left to her by her divine Master in order that she may meet them?

Let it be observed we are talking of power, not of ideas or plans or methods, but of genuine power.

Further, we are insisting that the Church needs power to meet these new challenges, not political power or material power but the power that is uniquely hers, the power of the Spirit of God.

Are we left to find out these things for ourselves? We would expect to find our highest leadership aware of the need and the answer. So let us hear Pope John XXIII:

> May there be repeated thus in the Christian families the spectacle of the Apostles, gathered together in Jerusalem after the Ascension of Jesus to heaven, when the new born Church was completely united in communion of thought and prayer with Peter and around Peter the shepherd of the lambs and the sheep. And may the Divine Spirit deign to answer in a most comforting manner the prayer that rises daily to Him from every corner of the earth: 'Renew your wonders in our time, as though for a new Pentecost and grant that the Holy Church, persevering in unanimous and continuous prayer, together with Mary, the mother of Jesus, and also under the guidance of Saint Peter, may increase the reign of the Divine Saviour, the reign of truth and justice, the reign of love and peace.[11]

This prayer, which, as the Pope indicates, expresses the aspirations of the whole Church, is being answered in a most striking fashion. Without doubt the Holy Spirit working

42

through the various agencies of the Church is renewing it at all
levels; not only at the highest levels, but also at the ground level
of the people of God, and perhaps more strikingly than ever
before. For whereas we recognise in earlier times the emergence
of a saint or saints or a pontiff, charged with a great task of
renewal, or the arrival of new religious orders with special con-
tributions to make, in this our time the Holy Spirit works directly among the people of God, encouraging them to seek anew the
fulness of His life and His gifts. As St Augustine of Hippo
suddenly recoiled in astonishment before God as the 'Beauty,
ever ancient and ever new', so today the most ordinary people
are given the overwhelming experience of God's power acting
through the Spirit of Christ, at once ever ancient in the Church
and ever new in our assemblies.

What God grants to us in this our harassed twentieth century is
not a new message, but the grace to be penetrated by the understanding and power of the same message.

Clearly such wonderful graces need to be sought under the
guidance of the leaders of the Church, that is, of the bishops.
Clearly too 'by their fruits you shall know them'; it is possible
for those who receive God's gifts to err, to fall away, to lead
others in false directions. But this is true of any and every movement in the Church. We cannot reject the Spirit of God because
some of us, poor human beings, get the message mixed up or
deliver it in odd terms.

There is nothing new, then, in praying with total sincerity
'Veni Sancte Spiritus', come, Holy Spirit. But He does some new
thing in each of us in answer to this prayer, and does some new
or renewed things in those Christian prayer meetings where all
are expectant of His manifestation and attentive to His inspirations.

These inspirations do not replace traditional Christian wisdom;
they do not take away from the appreciation of all that is given
in the Sacraments; on the contrary they confer a heightened sense
of such favours. Indeed, the realities of the Christian liturgy and
the traditional teachings of ascetical and mystical theology
receive a wonderful freshness from this action of the Holy Spirit.
To suppose otherwise would be to think that fire was the enemy
of fire.

What is here called the 'Newness of Life' is simply Christian life as received in the early Church, as carried forward by countless Christians in the succeeding ages, and now offered anew, with the strength and power necessary for our own difficult epoch, by the Holy Spirit himself. For each one of us it is 'new' even as, in the natural order, the being possessed by love for the first time is new for each human heart. But this newness of love is of the Spirit of God, and what may rightly cause us astonishment — but not disbelief — is the sheer liberality of God's giving, as if God said 'I have a special gift for your troubled times!'

It is the intention of the following pages to give him who turns to the Spirit for this grace, a little help in the understanding of the way along which he is being led. But since all depends on the action of the Holy Spirit within him, it is essential for him to spend such time as he can each day in the prayer of one who seeks.

From Day 4, the style of the writing will become more didactic while the examination of the charismatic renewal on the basis of Scripture is delineated.

Day 1: What is meant by life. What God intends

I shall put my spirit in you, and you shall live — it is I, the Lord Yahweh who speaks.

Ezek 37: 14

It is possible to work forwards or backwards, as we prefer: the message is the same. Ezekiel proclaimed a message of new life for his people, and for them it lay in the future; it was something mysterious, awaiting fulfilment. When Christ came He brought the message to fulfilment, saying 'This is fulfilled in me', and since He came, it is fulfilled ever anew. Hence we may see how,

44

with an astonishing new liberality, this fulfilment is being conferred in our own generation. Alternatively, if we start by recognising that God cleans, renews, puts a new heart and a new spirit into people and 'lives' in them in our own times, we shall have to transfer our thoughts back to the words of Christ, and see them literally interpreted by the Apostles, to understand this phenomenon. And finally we shall be led back to recognise the initial stage in which God spoke through the prophets centuries before Christ came. Either way we shall come to see the consistency with which God adheres to His loving message, and that it is meant also for us, provided we take Him at his word and will accept it.

Life is promised to us — something additional to that which God, equally freely, granted us in the first moment of our conception. Life is the dearest and deepest thing in us. It is in fact so central that we have to perceive it by its effects; hence we speak of a happy life, an unhappy life, a rich life, a poor life, a joyful life, an embittered life, for life itself is capable of infinite enrichment, or alas! of the most profound impoverishment or the most terrible distortion. This tends to hide from us that the ultimate good is life itself; if it does not seem to be so a warping and disfigurement has taken place, disguising the first gift and turning it to sadness. In Ezekiel's prophecy, God says that He will go to the very core and centre of man and change that; for it is out of this core that all good things in life spring. God alone has the power to make this change. And His reason for making it is that He loves and cherishes us, His people. He wants us to be His; He wants to be ours. But we are stony hearted,[1] unresponsive, leaden; He, who gave us the first life, has to stretch forth his finger again, touch, and transform us.

So our Saviour said 'I came so that they may have life and have it in abundance;[2] this life that He offers is something to be had now and abundantly or richly — as there is no need for poor men in the Kingdom of God; abundance is for all. It is not a question of fulfilling laws, having the right habits, saying one's prayers, going to church, keeping the ten Commandments, refraining from vice: all these things are necessary and are not to be abolished or even minimised. But the Lord's gift is *Life*, which is something deeper and more vital than all this.

Our life is what we value, love, know to be the realisation of ourselves and our personal gifts. God freely bestowed on us all that was necessary for life as one of His adopted children in our baptism: but often this gift has not developed into the fullness He intended; our development has been restricted and warped. Its fullness implies giving love with security, and receiving love with joy. No list of duties, however excellent and praiseworthy adds up to 'life'.

And life as God intended it to be is vibrant, pulsating with love given and received, rich with new and God-given experiences. And hence our Lord Himself, the giver of all these new riches, these new dimensions of happiness, this total change of what life is known and felt to be about – called it simple 'Life', and said He wanted us to have it in abundance. This undertaking on His part is of the greatest significance to those who have failed to grasp that His offering to us is precisely the gift of life: they think of their religion as the buying of the Kingdom of Heaven by instalments – church-going on Sunday, or a sufficient quantity of prayer, being instalments to be paid – with the premium to be claimed after death, provided of course that you don't fall down on the instalments. Hence they tend to think of God's commandments as inhibiting, as impoverishing life, since these commandments confine our freedom of choice, and warn us against giving ourselves up to the total enjoyment of the Now. It is then absolutely necessary to insist that it is *Life* that is being offered to us – and now. Some persons know this reality intellectually; they have read about it; but they need to feel its truth more fully in other parts of their make-up. It is not purely a matter of intellectual perception.

For this 'life' may be compared to a flame. Let us think of a gas water-heater. When the gas is turned down the flame may be reduced to a tiny little blue jet, giving neither light nor heat. Yet it is of infinite possibilities. If it is turned up there will be a blaze and hot water in no time at all. If it is out altogether it cannot be turned up, but needs to be relit. So is the divine activity within us. And the business in which we are now engaged may be likened to asking the Holy Spirit to turn up the little blue jet to full power; we cannot do this ourselves; but we can decide that we want it more than anything else. We can turn to God, exposing to Him our desire and such decision as we are capable of. He will then turn to us.

Day 2: The giving of life and the renewal of life

I live, and you will live.

John 14: 19

Of what precisely does this 'new life' consist? What does Our Lord mean when He says that He lives – and that we shall receive of this life?

Fundamentally all Christians who are baptised have received from God the gift of adoption; they are enrolled in the members of His own family as brothers of Christ. But God is a Spirit, and it is only by His activity within us that we can properly speak of a living presence. Baptism constitutes an irrevocable adoption on His side, and gives an unfailing right to claim the consequences of this adoption on ours. These consequences are His multiform activity through the Holy Spirit – an activity impossible without our co-operation – but, when that co-operation is given, producing a 'new man', so different will be his thoughts, desires, and hopes.

Although the thing we call 'life' cannot itself be felt in the natural order, but is experienced through its effects and treasured accordingly, so in the 'new life' there are effects to be experienced. Where there is no experience of any divine effects the life is in a very low state; somewhat as a human being in a coma would be in a poor state of life, although he might have a good brain and a full set of human capabilities. Such a one might well be alive, and yet we could speak quite intelligibly of his 'coming to life' again.

To be renewed in the Spirit is to come to life again. This will

47

show itself in certain characteristics, which were always potential growths from baptism, but which now start showing astonishing signs of animation.

For example, there will be a new set of interests, in the sense that there is a real discovery of Christ's interests, and that they are *interests*. Fundamentally Christ has two interests – perhaps 'passions' would be a better word for they consumed Him entirely. The first is the glory of God the Father. 'Father,' he said at the end of His life, 'I have glorified you on earth, and finished the work that you gave me to do'.[1] The second is the salvation of man, to which He referred saying 'I have come to bring fire to the earth, and how I wish it were blazing. There is a baptism I must still receive, and how great is my distress till it is over.'[2] This salvation of man is not to be conceived as instructions for a programme of good behaviour, or as a hurrying of the sinner past God's final judgement; it is far more, the realisation of much fruit.[3] He intends that we should enjoy even here below the realisation of our birthright as happy members of His family, learning as it were to bear the weight of all the joy that is to come.[4]

These new interests proceed from a new capacity to love, because one is newly aware of the quality of Christ's love. Look at any two lovers, and recognise that for them love is an entirely new thing; they are for themselves the first persons in the world to really understand the thing; for their love is first hand, unique, their own singular experience. And such is the love of Christ: it is unique, immediate, not depending upon any third party; and offered in a unique way to each person, so that it is completely personal, and yet not exclusive.

There will also be a new capacity to surrender oneself, and to accept the healing of one's wounds, for we are often badly damaged by life. Christ the Healer invites us to faith, and then says so simply to us 'Your faith has healed you'. Like hurt children we tend to shy away from the appearance of a doctor; we want to remain as we are rather than risk the pain of a cure. The quality of the life that Christ imparts to us is such that it overcomes not only death, of which it is the contrary, but those little deaths or diminishings or corruptions of our human personality which imply that something has died in us. Hence a

48

quality of this new life is that it brings with it a willingness to surrender the closed areas, the wounded places of our personality to the Divine Healer. He sends His Spirit, we know not how, and there is life where before there was sickness.

He offers us life. Let us make our decision and turn to Him for His promise, even as Scripture invites us.

Let us be confident, then, in approaching the throne of grace, that we shall have mercy from Him, and find grace when we are in need of help[4] – which is now. We shall find this confidence to which we are urged more easily, if we remind ourselves:

This promise was first announced by the Lord Himself
And guaranteed *to us* by those who heard Him.
God Himself confirmed their witness with signs and marvels and miracles of all kinds, and by *freely giving the gifts of the Holy Spirit.*[5]

And so God continues to confirm His promise in our days. Pray then with sincerity and with constancy that God may work these things in you. This prayer may help:

A pure heart create for me, O God,
Put a steadfast spirit within me:
Do not cast me away from Your presence
Nor deprive me of Your Holy Spirit.
Give me again the joy of Your help;
With a spirit of fervour sustain me.

Ps 51: 10-12

Day 3: The submission of the heart to Christ's authority

Jesus came up and spoke to them. He said 'All authority in heaven and on earth has been given to Me.'

Mt 28: 18

49

Thus, after the Resurrection, Jesus spoke to his disciples and declared to them the fruits gained on behalf of all humanity by His victory on the Cross.

It is our part simply to accept this authority. For some this may not be so easy, since the very word 'authority' conveys to them an unhappy idea of coercion. But there will be no coercion here. Others may feel that they have always accepted His authority, yet have to learn that there are areas of their personality which are withdrawn from full submission, or even any submission to His authority.

For all of us it is a question of accepting anew, as not hitherto, the fullness of His authority, and declaring Him to be our Lord. The capacity to say 'Jesus is Lord' was the test by which the acceptance of the Good News was measured in the primitive Church.[1] Nor should we underestimate what was – and is – involved. The depth with which we acknowledge it rather than the loudness with which we proclaim it, is the measure of our submission to His authority. Indeed it is when it is proclaimed externally, without submission of the heart, that we get the all too common phenomenon we call 'nominal Christianity' or 'nominal Catholicism'.

It is an authority which has to be received into our inmost parts, the most secret passages of our mind, the most hidden of our desires. It is not a matter of external control, but of acceptance into our heart of His love as our rule of life. And it is possible because Christ sends His Spirit into our hearts so that we desire just this thing.

Consider also the little matter of time. God does not keep us in being on a part time basis. Christ does not love us part of the time. The Holy Spirit has no specific hours of occupation, as sometimes He astonishingly demonstrates. For this reason St Paul did not hesitate to describe himself as a slave (*doulos*) of the Gospel; for a slave has no free time, he cannot down tools after an eight hour day, there is no part of his existence he can call his own. So, – but how gently! – we are invited to turn ourselves to serve Christ, to admit His Spirit into our hearts, to worship the Father in Spirit and truth. This does not mean, of course, that we have to spend the day on our knees; but it does mean that the Spirit of God is ever with us, and keeps us conscious of the sweet authority of Christ our Master in all that we have to do or say or think.

With this activity of the Holy Spirit we have to co-operate to the best of our ability. We have not in ourselves the power to do this completely, and we should deceive ourselves if we thought otherwise; for nothing less than a conversion of all our actions through the influence of love for God is implied. This is an undertaking the implications of which God reveals to us little by little. At the beginning it is rather as if He said 'I have many things to say to you, but you cannot bear them now!' (John 16:12) It is enough then that we turn to Him in simple confidence and with a deep desire, and say 'Yes, Lord I will. Be Thou my Lord in all things.' After that He comes immediately to our aid.

We shall perhaps find it easier to do this if we recall that we place ourselves fully under His authority in order that, being accepted as Our Lord, He may work in us His will, which is life-giving beyond conception; we need healing, and saving and fulfilment. And this is what He wants to bring us. If we submit to Him, we must not think of Him as we would of a human person in power. Unlike a human being He does not issue orders to be obeyed; He makes known His invitations, and sends His Spirit into hearts, so that we may both desire to fulfil those invitations and have the power to do so. Moreover this ownership of His – for that is what we make over to Him – is a deep taking of possession; and this is the source of all joy.

It is true of course of any good Christian that the Holy Spirit dwells within him by a degree of activity. But there are various degrees, as there are also barriers (of which more later). What we have to aim at now is to collect ourselves, so to speak, to make a deliberate and total surrender to the Lordship of Christ, so that He, taking possession, may send His Spirit into our hearts to a degree hitherto unknown to us.[2] Then we shall find obedience to His will no longer a submission, counter to what we really want, to one who seems to be outside us; but we shall find that our will is to do His will. And with some effort on our part, this will grow. Our sadness is that we have not done His will with so much of our lives. This sadness, with His aid, we put behind us.

51

Day 4: This promise is for you

When Pentecost day came round, they were all filled with the Holy Spirit, and began to speak in tongues as the Spirit gave them the gift of speech.

Acts 2: 1, 4

The group referred to is that described in *Acts* 1: 14:[1] the Apostles, the devout women (presumably the little group that had followed Him from Galilee and shared so closely in His crucifixion, entombment and resurrection), Mary His mother and His brethren or relatives. Already at the Last Supper, Our Lord had promised them that He would send His Spirit saying: 'I shall ask the Father and He will give you another advocate to be with you for ever, the Spirit of truth.'[2] And just before He left them He instructed them not to leave Jerusalem but to wait 'for what the Father had promised'. 'It is' He had said 'what you have heard me speak about: John baptised with water; not many days from now, you will be baptised with the Holy Spirit'.[3] It was in fact just ten days that they had to wait, and to persevere in prayer. Then with the sound of a mighty wind and under the appearance of fire the Spirit filled each of them, and was seen to rest like a tongue of fire on the head of each man and woman present.

Nothing in their Master's discourse had really prepared them for this phenomenon. For indeed nothing can bridge such a gap between personal impotence and indwelling power. And if the passion and death of Christ had shattered their belief in Christ as the restorer of the Kingdom of Israel, the joy of the Resurrection had not changed fundamentally their immaturity of outlook. Now by a mighty invasion of divine power came the Holy Spirit to fulfil the promise of Christ, to cleanse, enlighten, fortify, fulfil and strengthen them. They reeled under the impact and gave vent to loud and joyful cries in praise of God. They came out of the house, stumbling and staggering, dazed, and uttering loudly their cries of praise. To make it even odder it was observed that each of the crowd seemed to hear them in his own language; a crowd had come hurrying up to find out what the noise of a powerful wind swirling round a particular house might signify. When the Apostles came stumbling out the first effect on the onlookers was puzzlement . . . followed by a good laugh. 'They have been drinking too much new wine' they said. They knew the symptoms – the stumbling gait, the uncontrolled speech, the dazed condition. Yet if some of the results could thus be explained, they remained amazed; obviously something unusual had happened.

So St Peter, a new Peter, quite different from the one who had cringed under questioning in the high priest's palace a few weeks before, spoke up for the others. He began modestly enough. 'These men are not drunk as you imagine . . .' that is to say, in the way that the spectators imagined, but because of the outpouring of the Spirit.

St Peter, having explained the nature of the phenomenon as the fulfilment of the prophecy of Joel, made four significant points in his sermon:

1. Let them all know for certain that Jesus whom they had crucified was the Lord and the Christ;

2. They should repent and change their hearts;

3. They should be baptised in the name of Jesus Christ for the forgiveness of their sins, and would then receive the gift of the Holy Spirit.

4. This promise that was made is for you and your children, and for all those who are far away, for all those whom God will call to Himself.[4]

We also must reckon ourselves among 'those far away' and we have exactly the same programme laid before us. Firstly, to believe, to commit ourselves completely to Jesus our Saviour. Secondly, to repent or to turn away from all that holds us back, to seek new conversion; thirdly, to be baptised (unless that has already been done), and to receive the gift of the Holy Spirit.

Yes, it may seem puzzling that if we have already been baptised, which implies the reception of the Holy Spirit (even as the

Sacrament of Confirmation implies a further stage in the same process), how is it that we seem not to have received the Spirit? Without question, we received the Spirit of God in baptism, and baptism cannot be repeated. The explanation is that by this new reception the effects of the sacrament will be kindled anew, actuated anew. Yet it is not a returning to the condition of one newly baptized, but rather a new effusion of the Spirit, such as we have not known before, for which baptism provides the basis.

This implies no lack of significance in God's previous gift to us. On the contrary, it is by virtue of that gift that we may confidently expect its activation. We turn to God with a new expectancy, and prepare ourselves for a yet fuller grace, the enjoyment of the powers that are already given, which lie like a gift still inside its wrapper.

Shall we call it a gift for our own times? For in our times man has developed his knowledge and power over God's material gifts in the universe, often to the great neglect of the giver. So God steps forward again saying: See, I send my Spirit anew to work new wonders among you, to pick up the sorrowful, to reanimate the weary, to touch the cynical, to heal the bitter, to give power to the weak.

And so in our days the Church rejoices in the renewal of the gifts of the Spirit throughout its members. We have but to come, to accept, and to drink of the flowing waters of this divine new largesse.

This promise is for you ... and for all those whom God will call to Himself. Consider in prayer the significance of St Peter's words and the content of what he refers to as The Promise. Is there not more for you here, and do you not need this 'more'?

Day 5: Baptism and spiritual gifts

Every one of you must be baptised in the name of Jesus Christ for the forgiveness of your sins, and you will receive the gift of the Holy Spirit.

Acts 2:38

St Peter alludes to two things which recur in the *Acts* as operations that went to the making of new Christians: baptism, and the conferring of the gift of the Holy Spirit. Baptism was in itself the the essential conferring of the Holy Spirit; yet there were other gifts, signs of His presence, awaiting the converts; gifts of the kind which Peter and the other Apostles had just received, and which were in some way visible or perceptible by others.

From the *Acts* we conclude that such additional gifts usually appeared after baptism, but not always. For we are shown cases when the gifts of the Spirit are given before baptism and after baptism, as well as at baptism. So the distinction cannot be doubted, nor that the Apostles were conscious of power to give these gifts.

The conferring of spiritual gifts before baptism must have been unusual. Perhaps the Holy Spirit wished to demonstrate that He was subject to no law. Such was the case of Cornelius the centurion. Peter had barely finished explaining why it would be right to admit Cornelius to the Church when 'the Holy Spirit came down on all the listeners', to the astonishment of Peter's Jewish companions who 'could hear them speaking strange tongues and proclaiming the greatness of God'. Nothing remained but to baptise them. But the order of events was certainly unusual.[1]

On the other hand, when the Apostles heard that the converts of Philip the deacon in Samaria had been baptised, but that in spite of the miracles and wonders which accompanied Philip's evangelisation, these converts had not received the Holy Spirit ('for as yet He had not come down on any of them'), they sent Peter and John down to them. 'They laid hands on them, and they received the Holy Spirit.'[2] The resulting signs are not described, but they were so effective that a certain Simon, by trade a magician, wanted to buy the power for himself. In this case there was an interval between the two events, and the ministers of each are different.

But the commonest happening would seem to be that described as taking place later at Ephesus. Here Paul found devout men, converts apparently, who had accepted Christ on the strength of the teaching of John the Baptist; they had also received John's baptism, and then presumably returned to their homes at Ephesus. So Paul completed their instruction, and 'they were baptised in the name of the Lord Jesus, and the moment Paul had laid hands on them, the Holy Spirit came down on them, and they began to speak in tongues and to prophesy'.[3]

The overall impression is that baptism and a conferring of special gifts with the laying on of hands as an accompanying gesture, went together.

These special gifts have never died out in the Church. But they have become much less frequent, and among Catholics have been associated with personal sanctity in the person exercising them. It is clear that no such association is to be found in the New Testament, where these gifts are showered on beginners. In the quotations just cited from the *Acts* it seems clear that the Holy Spirit fell upon quite ordinary persons, who then showed themselves 'full of the Spirit'. This did not mean that the full internal harmony which we associate with Christian sanctity had already been conferred on them. They received wonderful gifts, astonishing signs, and these signs were conferred to show unmistakably that God had accepted them, and was working in them, confirming their faith, giving them wonderful joy, and a perception of the reality of being transferred from the kingdom of darkness to the Kingdom of Christ. But these gifts did not remove the need to grow spiritually, nor the necessity to do battle with human defects, nor did they imply full spiritual maturity. Indeed we know that the Christians of Corinth, although rich in spiritual gifts, were not characterised by spiritual maturity: St Paul, in his own language, had given them only 'spiritual milk', for they could not take stronger food.[4] But the gifts brought them an experience of Christ's power over the kingdom of darkness, over wickedness in all its forms; they brought great joy, and were to be used for the building up of the Church.

An exact definition of the baptism in the Spirit is a difficult matter on account of the great variety of its effects, and also because we are not well informed as to the procedures of the early Church. It may be useful to note that when St Luke refers to the phenomena that followed baptism, he seems mainly concerned with the demonstration of the power of the Spirit in new Christians, and that it is this demonstration of power that witnesses to the truth of the Gospel, and affects those who see and hear it. The fact that this is still true – that people in general are deeply impressed by the manifestation in human beings of the power of God – is one reason why the charismatic movement grows apace.

Pray then that God may lead you to a knowledge of His power not as an abstract proposition, but as something exercised in ordinary persons.

Day 6: The meaning of baptism in the Spirit

But you, not many days from now, will be baptised with the Holy Spirit.

Acts 1:5

It is from this text that the expression 'baptism of the Spirit' draws its origin. It may be defined as an experienced spiritual renewal, worked by the Holy Spirit within a person.[1] In the case of Christians, it is an actualisation, a bringing to blossom and to fruit of the divine life conferred originally at baptism, and carried forward by confirmation and the eucharist. It does not conflict with these sacraments, nor overshadow them; it brings about their experienced fulfilment. This fulfilment sometimes starts with a strong, vivid, powerful experience, which will in itself not continue, but leaves behind its effects, and provides the basis for a renewed life with Christ. On the other hand the 'baptism of the Spirit' may appear to have little effect, there is little or no emotional impact at the time, but there starts a progress that will gather in power. It is as if someone of immense power were to put his shoulder to a heavy vehicle; at first it moves very slowly, but there is a growing facility, an increasing mobility; it gathers speed as the power takes effect. We can say that the operation we call the baptism of the Spirit works one of these two ways – taking them as extremes, with other possibilities lying in between. But also the baptism of the Spirit usually brings with it, either at once or later, spiritual gifts, either felt interiorly, or manifesting themselves exteriorly.

But why does the Holy Spirit perform these operations precisely in our own times? There is no reason for supposing that He confines His operations to our times; but the liberality of grace seems marked in our times; there is ample evidence of its widespread outpouring. And it is an outpouring resembling the experience of the early Church; it is not confined to persons who have attained holiness, but is offered freely to all; reminding us of the parable of the sower who went forth to sow, and cast his seed all over the place. But why, then, this astonishing liberality in our own times? The answer seems to be: We need it. The difficulties standing in the way of Christian faith in our own pagan times are comparable to the difficulties facing the primitive Church. We need God's gifts as much as the members of that church did. How could they set about the task of convincing a cultured pagan world that their crucified Jewish prophet was the source of all salvation? It was laughable. How shall a modern Christian reply to the vast advances in science and technology which dissolve the cement of society, the traditional views of life's significance and accepted ethics, all around him? He is at a loss. He may be a priest; he is still at a loss. He may be a theologian, but the world is not looking to him for answers. Only the Holy Spirit can by His power give the Christian that full certainty, security and joy, which he needs in the world of today. That is why God, who is ever with His Church in her hour of need, and equally ever with man in his hour of anxiety, invites us – by the manifestation of His power to renew us – to turn to Him again.

This then is why the 'baptism of the Spirit' is offered us now. Normally now – as in earlier times – it is transacted by a laying on of hands, preceded by a praying together. This can be done either with the aid of one who has already received the Spirit, or more commonly with the aid of a group or community who are already so gifted. This last procedure has the advantage that a group that has already acquired a diversity of gifts and made a kind of collective spiritual progress, seems to combine the individual strengths of its members into a powerful communal prayer. Either way is possible, or neither – for it is by no means unknown for the Holy Spirit to respond to an intense desire by a sudden and powerful coming without making use of any third party.

It is desirable to stress one thing. We are all invited to receive this blessing, but it is not a magical operation. It is a prayer in faith. It is important before we seek it that we prepare ourselves well, both by acquiring the necessary knowledge as to what it is about, and by preparing the necessary dispositions in our soul: these include, faith, expectancy, humility.

'The wind blows wherever it pleases:
You hear its sound,
but you cannot tell where it comes from or where it is going.
That is how it is with all who are born of the Spirit.'[2]

This comparison with the wind is illuminating. For the wind varies from a mighty force to a gentle breeze that picks up a little leaf and blows it slowly along. It is not a man-made force, it is not controlled by man; it cannot be seen, only felt. Man can harness its power so that it drives ships or turns mills, but fundamentally the wind is the master, man the one who accepts. This comparison with the wind is set forth by our Lord Himself, He warns us emphatically that we can only accept the Spirit, not expect to control Him; hear His voice, but not decide His direction. He directs us.

The essence then of this phenomenon is the taking possession of us, how precisely we cannot say; it is done gently or more vigorously, as He wills. There are signs of this taking possession – phenomena such as the speaking in tongues, prophecy – they are like the phenomena that result from a wind; they may be great or small. For a wind may wave a leaf gently or bring down a wall. But always the Spirit Himself is the first gift; always there are certain unmistakable signs of His presence. These signs of His presence may be the answer to an individual's personal needs, or they may be gifts intended for the building up of the community.

Day 7: The effects of baptism in the Spirit

I would have you aglow with the Spirit

Rom 12:11 (Knox tr.)

The act known as the 'baptism of the Spirit' or, better, 'the release of the Spirit' needs to be seen in perspective, not as an end in itself but as a fresh start.

When we seek this act of renewal, the release of the Spirit, it should not be our aim only to have an experience of extraordinary joy — a spiritual summit, so to speak.

Nor should we expect to enter on a state of spiritual euphoria, seeing the world henceforward through rose-tinted spectacles.

Still less should we hope only to acquire some remarkable gift, such as speaking in tongues, or prophecy or healing. We should be not far from the attitude of Simon Magus [7] if that was our main intention!

What we should seek is to be allowed in the mercy and love and power of God to be admitted to the experience of a new relationship with Him — in the sense that we hope and expect to become conscious, as He wills, in whatever way He wills, that His Spirit is at work within us, has taken us at our word, and is changing us with His power, and drawing us closer into oneness with Christ.

'Taken us at our word.' This is important. For our word must be the desire, amounting to a decision based on faith, to give over the control of our life to His abiding presence. There must be a deep turning to Him so that He may take possession of us. It is true that we may not feel capable of any depth at all; we do our

60

best. And it is true that we can only make ourselves over as we are; He knows that too.

The praying over us, or the imposition of hands is not then a consummation but an invitation. It is the beginning of the life that we shall lead renewed by God's Spirit. It is only right that we should prepare ourselves for it by knowledge and the right dispositions as well as we can.

The observable effects, the gifts immediately perceived, vary enormously. For some there is an overwhelming experience, for others there is no emotional or psychological sensation at all. But provided that the right dispositions are there and preparation has been made, effects will follow as the Spirit intends, and indeed (such is the goodness of God) these will frequently be discovered to be what in our deepest heart we wanted Him to do for us, or correspond to what we had desired to do for Him. But the important thing is to want His gift, not our own choosing.

Apart from the specific 'charismatic gifts' and fruits to be examined later, the following effects may be anticipated:[2]

1. A profounder knowledge or experience that one is a son of God, with all this implies.

2. The experience that prayer becomes easier, more intimate, more attractive, for no discernible cause. (The actual cause is that the Spirit is doing the work within us.)

3. With this may come a sudden sense of our responsibility to pray for other people, or a realisation that we are surrounded by people whom we can help. This help may be by our prayers, or by the use of natural gifts which so far have lain idle. We realise too that suffering persons make a call on us – as they did on Christ.

4. It is a common testimony that the Bible 'comes alive'; that texts which we have frequently read without great interest suddenly shout at us. Obviously this supposes that we do read the Bible and consecrate time to this necessary act. But from a recognised duty it becomes an object of desire.

5. There may be an increase of joy, or at least a sense of tranquillity, that is, in embryo, the peace of Christ. If we correspond, the Spirit will fan this flame, and it will grow to a strong flame. As has already been indicated, for some there will be a strong start, for others a gentle growth. It is well to bear in mind that

sometimes the Spirit holds back experience, in order that we may stand in faith and expectancy until His moment comes. And then the gift will be given more strongly.

6. There is also an inner healing and cleansing which is inevitable when the Spirit comes in power. There may however be obstacles in us, not deliberately opposed ones, but the effects of long formed mental habits of our own remembered past. The cleansing may be a gradual ongoing process to which we have to correspond; but sometimes it is sudden, even overwhelming.

No one is sent empty away. The thirsty are not invited to come and drink in order to be told that they are not included in the invitation list. No one need fear that God will not take him at his word, or that he will remain unnoticed, untouched, out of contact with the God to whom he turns. God's promises stand for all who seek Him; the only condition is that we seek Him in spirit and in truth.

Some share in the gifts of the Spirit may be expected with confidence, but we should understand these gifts or charismata in the fullness of their range, and not simply as preternatural phenomena making one a rather special person. We are each special enough before God, but we must not have narrow ideas of the gifts that He wills to give. We don't need to be special before men.

Week four: Rich in Christ

This week requires little introduction, but it brings us to the heart of the matter.

In the last week the theme of the meditations was the significance of 'newness of life' in Christ Jesus and what we mean by renewal. This week investigates in outline how this renewal brings spiritual gifts enriching the receiver.

The variety of lists may seem confusing, yet it is important to distinguish those effects of the gifts of the Spirit which properly enrich all souls as a result of baptism, the growing harvest of virtue which sprouts from this initial giving, and finally those gifts which are given for the sake of others, and are sometimes called 'ministerial gifts', since they enable us to minister one to another.

If not much is said about prayer-meetings and life in community, it is not intended in any way to underestimate the significance of either. But it is presumed that those who are following these pages are not in a position to receive personal instruction. Hence the somewhat individualist approach. That the life in the Spirit calls for community life and a spiritual sharing one with another, as far as human circumstances permit, is not to be doubted.

Also, the life in the Spirit is not to be thought of as 'tied' to a certain type of prayer meeting.

Day 1: The fruit of the Spirit

The fruit* of the Spirit is love, joy, peace, patience, kindness, generosity, faithfulness, gentleness, self-control

Gal 5:22-23

Here St Paul lists some of the most important effects of the work of the Spirit in us. He calls them the 'fruit', implying that they all grow together and are not to be thought of as separated. Moreover the fact that fruit *grows* indicates that it is not of our manufacturing. We cannot create such qualities; we cannot even augment them. The Kingdom of Heaven is like the seed which a man casts into a field, 'night and day, it grows, *he knows not how'.*[1] Man does not provide the dynamic vital force by which God's fruit grows, any more than he provides the original seed. All is of God, though all calls for the co-operation of man. We shall bear these fruits because the Spirit is alive within us; and they will grow as we surrender more to the divine Gardener. It is His vineyard; the fruits are for Him; He wants a good crop.

These fruits are different in kind from the 'gifts' referred to in I *Cor* 12:4-11, which are 'ministries', or powers to be used directly for the building up of the Church of God. They are in themselves very intimate qualities of the soul by which it reflects the goodness of God, and rejoices in Him. It is of such fruits that our Lord said 'By their fruits you shall know them'[2], for when these qualities are discernible, then surely is the Holy Spirit at work.

No list of this kind in Scripture is to be considered as complete and exhaustive; rather, the virtues referred to are mentioned as samples of the changes that the Spirit works in us. But other fruits could be mentioned. For example, how clear it is from *Acts* (chapter 2) that St Peter received a spirit of courage and boldness in proclaiming the Good News, such as he had not had before. And this was exactly what he needed; for he had the task of proclaiming that the man who had just been crucified by the joint authority of what we should call church and state was no

*The New English Bible translates 'the harvest of the Spirit . . . .'

less than the chosen one of God and the Lord of all. Freedom or a sense of liberation from the infestation of evil power is another fruit of the Spirit, and indeed any good and lovely quality that God produces in a human soul may be so described.

When we desire the 'release of the Spirit' we desire then that He should increase these fruits and any others that He wills in our souls. He will not be slow to do so, provided we oppose no barriers. Indeed much of our slow growth in the things that are pleasing to God is due to the fact that we do not desire to receive nearly as much as He desires to give; or that our desires are conditional rather than absolute.

Although these fruits are deep interior qualities enriching the receiver, yet they are not inward-looking. They originate in God's action within us to create a new relationship with our fellow men. Do not love, joy, peace, patience, kindness, generosity, self-control manifestly create a new and God-given relationship to our neighbour? And one that is devoid of the pretence which is so common a feature of our ordinary social relationships? It is devoid of all pretence because it proceeds from qualities that are transparently real, true love for our neighbour, true joy in our heart creating a feeling of desiring to give what has been so freely given to us, true peace because the egoistic motives for battle have vanished, true patience and not mere toleration, and a steady kindness; for are we not conscious of receiving the kindness of our God every moment of our lives?

Faithfulness here is that quality or fruit that really believes and trusts God, and accepts His will and praises Him, when the circumstances of life might prompt a very different reaction. It is the quality that, by absolute trust, overcomes and knows that God on His side is ever faithful and full of loving kindness.

A word about self-control. It is sometimes translated 'chastity', which is certainly a most intimate form of self-control. Unfortunately chastity is a matter which for some people seems beyond reach, and even for some devout people is almost a source of torment. They feel that they have lost it, that they can't recover it, or can't recover from the effects of having lost it. And they are sad. Being joyless, they are drawn to seek liberation where it is not to be found. But the Spirit can heal this emotional starvation by the infusion of His love. And by this healing He sets them on the road to recovery. There may be a battle with infesting evil spirits who do not want to release their prey, but the victory over them will follow by the strength of the same power of God.

Pray today that God may increase this harvest in your soul, and consider carefully the beauty of each of these promised qualities.

Day 2: The gifts of the Spirit

There is a variety of gifts, but always the same Spirit; there are all sorts of service to be done, but always the same Lord. . . . The particular way in which the Spirit is given to each person is for a good purpose. One may have the gift of preaching with wisdom given him by the spirit, another may have the gift of preaching instruction given him by the same Spirit; another again the gift of healing through this one Spirit; one the power of miracles; another prophecy; another the gift of recognising spirits; another the gift of tongues, and another the ability to interpret them. All these are the work of one and the same Spirit, who distributes different gifts to different people just as He chooses.

I Cor 12: 4-11

St Paul was writing to explain to the Corinthians the nature of the spiritual gifts they had received; he had an eye also to settling minor disturbances in the assemblies or prayer meetings. He would have been greatly surprised to find that he had raised far more controversy than he had settled, more surprised still to find that these matters could become the core of so much dispute between types of Christian! He did his best to show the Corinthians that they were not the core of Christian spirituality and yet that they had their purpose: they were for these converts the demonstration of the Holy Spirit's reality and power, they were the source of immense joy, they built up, as he explains, the mystical Body of Christ.

Nor in fact has Christ ever left His Church without perceptible demonstrations of divine power. They have always been there, always understood by some and always ignored and rejected by others. Since now God manifests Himself anew by broadcasting His power through the conferring of these gifts on ordinary people, let us examine them and see what they are about.

Firstly observe the expression 'all sorts of service to be done', or as in other translations 'all sorts of ministries'. These gifts then are primarily outward looking, for the building up of the Church as a whole; different persons will be given different gifts for this purpose, not as a tribute to their own excellence.

The list is not exhaustive; and there are other lists.[1] Nor is there total agreement on the significance of one or two. Moreover they are not all abnormal phenomena. To speak in tongues is a phenomenon that stands out from normal behaviour patterns; 'preaching with wisdom' does not imply such abnormality, yet it is equally given by the Holy Spirit. By definition then a 'charisma' is not just something extraordinary or abnormal, nor even an abnormal power given by the Spirit – it is simply a gift of the Spirit, which may or may not seem abnormal, but is in fact a true gift from Him and not to be accounted for by human effort. Human effort may well go into preaching, but there is a charism or gift of the Spirit which makes it something more.

Hence it would be (in the words of Fr Yves Congar) 'an intolerable abuse' to confine our use of the word 'charismatic' to this list of ministries, which in fact refers mainly to the supernatural phenomena brought into play by the early Christian assemblies. We have always to remember that the Holy Spirit can and does give charismatic power and guidance to all the functions of the Christian life that call for it and to all persons who will admit it. One filled with the Spirit might actually not have any of the above nine gifts – and yet have others more particularly required by his position in the Church. St Paul makes this clear when he numbers administration among the tasks to be performed by the aid of the Spirit:

'Our gifts differ according to the grace given us. If your gift is prophecy, then use it as your faith suggests, if administration, then use it for administration; if teaching, then use it for teaching. Let the preachers deliver sermons, almsgivers give freely, the officials be diligent, and those who do works of mercy, do them cheerfully.'[2]

This is not just moral advice; it is, as with the other text, instruction in how to lead the life in the Spirit. The essential is that what we do, whatever our function is, shows forth powerfully the working of the Holy Spirit within us. Some of the gifts take the form of special ministries for use in a Christian assembly; but the common factor in all recipients of charismata is that they have 'tasted of the gift of Heaven and received a share of the Holy Spirit, and appreciated the good message of God and the powers of the world to come.'[3]

And what finally do we understand by each of these nine gifts? An examination shows that they divide into three categories:[4]

1. The gift of preaching with wisdom; this refers to the power of penetration into doctrine, and consequent capacity to explain it in depth. It is not just human learning or human skill, but a super-added divine gift.

2. The gift of preaching instruction, or as sometimes translated 'the word of knowledge' applies not so much to any doctrine as to the need of a particular person or the need in a particular case. The person who has this gift is enabled to come up with the answer that is wanted.

These belong together; in a second category belong those gifts which call forth God's power and goodness. They enable us to call on God with confidence and in loving humility to manifest His care in a given situation. These are

3. 'The gift of faith, given by the same Spirit.'

4. The gift of healing through this one Spirit;

5. '. . . the power of miracles.'

These are clearly powers no one should seek for his own sake. The faith referred to is that which suddenly asserts itself at a given moment, knowing that God will answer our prayer; the answer will not necessarily be what we technically call a miracle, but those concerned will recognise it as the answer given by

God. The work of healing is now often carried on by a team, so that their diverse gifts may coalesce. At the root of the gift of healing lies a sharing in the compassion of Christ. For Catholics there is nothing new in the idea of miracles, but the Church has always been slow to commit herself offically in a given case. This does not mean that we should fail to interest ourselves in this power, which clearly can be of great use to the Church of God. Indeed we may say that if faith is deep, confidence is full, humility is complete . . . then God has not changed, and the power of Christ is not cut down. It is cut down only by our lack of faith in it.

The remaining four gifts, prophecy, discernment, speaking in tongues, interpretations, are all gifts by which God enriches the community through some form of revelation; either by His goodness, or His presence, or something that they are to learn, or that a single person is to learn. Prophecy does not necessarily concern the future: the prophet is one who speaks as he is inspired by God to speak. The corollary of prophecy may be discernment of spirits (the gift of recognising spirits). For in itself prophecy can be true, false, or simply null and void (the prophecy of someone who deceives himself without evil intent). Obviously false prophecy, such as Our Lord foretold would come, is extremely dangerous to the Christian community,[5] but true prophecy is a great gift, especially commended by St Paul.[6]

The gift of the interpreter is the gift of being able to state or interpret what a speaker in tongues has said. It is not a case of translating, as if the interpreter understood the language as such, but a specific gift by which he is able to state the content of the message, whatever the tongue used may be. Occasionally the tongue is a living recognisable one, but mostly it is not so. The interpreter is not infallible, and the use of his gift sometimes calls for courage.

Finally, there is the gift of tongues. As it is the commonest, the most discussed, and the most misunderstood, an examination of it is best left till tomorrow.

Day 3: Speaking in tongues

Do all speak strange languages, and all interpret them? I Cor 12: 30
I should like you all to have the gift of tongues. I Cor 14: 5

It may seem strange that St Paul, who has apparently rejected the idea that all should speak in tongues: 'Do all speak in tongues?'[1] because different persons have different functions to fulfil in one body, soon afterwards appears to indicate that the gift of tongues is something he desires for all (though he goes on to say, he desires the gift of prophecy yet more).

There is more than one explanation of St Paul's question. There can be the person who has the gift of tongues as a personal gift (i.e., it is not for everybody) and the person on whom it comes only occasionally, and is not thought of as endowed with a permanent gift.

Moreover the gift of tongues has a dual use. It may be used in an assembly; in this respect it is not requisite for all, and it is desirable that interpreters be present. Or it may be used simply to praise God or intercede with Him by oneself in private, since essentially it is a prayer-gift. Thus, anyone with the gift of tongues speaks to God, and this he can do very profitably at home.

St Paul is well aware of the limitations of this gift of the Spirit. 'Any uninitiated people or unbelievers coming into a meeting of the whole Church, where everybody was speaking in tongues, would say that you were mad'[2] or worse; 'If I am ignorant of what the sounds mean, I am a savage to the man who is speaking, and he is a savage to me.'[3] Many people today reproduce just these attitudes when they hear of charismatic meetings and speaking in tongues. It seems to them unnecessary, queer, suspicious — and useless. In fact they repeat as denunciations or expressions of disapproval what St Paul said by way of warning and instruction to the Corinthians.

Why then does the Spirit confer the gift of tongues? Why did St Paul make use of it himself,[4] and, after noting its limitations and place in the hierarchy of spiritual gifts, desire that the Corinthians, and presumably not them only, should speak in tongues?

The gift of speaking in a tongue or tongues is not essentially a prophecy or a revelation, but a gift of prayer. It is therefore primarily personal, though it may also be used in community. Of what use is it?

1. It is frequently accompanied by great spiritual joy, produced in the speaker by the Spirit.

2. By the very fact that the organs of speech control are surrendered to the control of the Spirit, it is a testimony to the presence and uplifting power of the Spirit in that person at that moment.

3. We do not always know how to make the best prayers — neither as to choosing our words, nor directing our intentions. But the Spirit does. No one could explain this more clearly than St Paul: 'For when we cannot choose words in order to pray properly, the Spirit himself expresses our plea in a way that could never be put into words, and God who knows everything in our hearts, knows perfectly well what He means, and the pleas of the saints expressed by the Spirit are according to the mind of God.'[5]

4. When used in an assembly in the way St Paul prescribes, with order and humility, it has a powerful effect on all. Newcomers may be alarmed; others know — the witness of their senses tells them — that the Spirit is at work, declaring Himself in their midst. Their deep reaction is an immediate 'Praise be to God, who has demonstrated His presence!'

Sometimes speech in tongues takes the form of singing in tongues. This can in itself be very beautiful. Sometimes this singing in tongues possesses those of the assembly (who are so gifted) simultaneously. It is a remarkable phenomenon since each uses his own tongue, and melody; yet the result is not a cacophony. There is a deep feeling that the Spirit has manifested Himself.

Such is the phenomenon known as 'glossolalia', which in no way lies at the heart of the charismatic movement, but does seem to be an invariable accompaniment.

St Paul would have spurned the idea that it was his business to impede or confine the coming of the Spirit, of whom he said that He distributes His gifts as He chooses Himself. St Paul congratulates the Corinthians on all that they had received;[6] he says that they were not without any gift of the Spirit; but he also had to clear up false impressions[7] as to the significance of these

71

spiritual gifts; and to introduce rather more order into the way they were used. He found the recipients, or some of them, immature but would not for that reason, 'extinguish the Spirit'[8]. He gave them a valuable lesson in the theology of the matter, and taught them how to keep a calm and orderly assembly.

It should be added that in fact audible glossolalia occupies but a small part in time of the ordinary charismatic meeting. Anyone who goes to a meeting thinking to find an orgy of strange phenomena is likely to be disappointed. Yet the gift of speaking in tongues is actually very common.

Day 4: Love – Healing – Power

I will pour my Spirit on all mankind.

Joel 3: 28

Over the past few days we have examined
1. the nature of what is called 'baptism of the Spirit' or the 'release of the Spirit', and of the ensuing life in the Spirit;
2. the fruit of the Spirit, those virtues that blossom under his life-giving touch:
3. the ministerial gifts of the Spirit, by which the members of the Church are enabled to help one another either by the conferring of a new power or the Spirit's strengthening their ability to do what it is their task to do already.

It may be useful now to consider that there are certain areas of our personality in which we are most helpless, and which are precisely those in which the Spirit delights to manifest Himself. In some way they concern all of us, as St Peter made clear, for he not only cited the above text and said 'This is being fulfilled today', he went on to underline the words 'on *all* mankind', by adding 'This promise is for you, for your children, and for all those far away, for all those whom the Lord our God will call to himself '.[1]

Which, then, are those parts of our personality which we may expect confidently that the Spirit will penetrate? Nothing can be excluded, but we shall not go wrong if we think in the first place of our needs in respect of love, healing and power. They are a trio interconnected among themselves, each one having its action on the other, and all proceeding from the action of the Spirit.

1. Love. Some people are blessed with a great and satisfying human love; some have the great blessing of a home in which love has been the common currency. But not all; far from it. Too often the grown person is greatly in need of love, would be a different person if he or she knew himself or herself as truly and deeply loved. Many having had their deep disappointments and accepted that love is not coming their way, have become unable to love. They dare not love, for experience deeper than conscious thought asserts that their love will not be returned. So they become frozen, frustrated, embittered; sometimes they show this – or rather hide this – by cynicism. Thus the door is locked; no love will issue from this heart, for it is too dangerous; no love is expected to knock on the door, for experience has taught the opposite. So the life dries up. And even if the person is a spiritual person, they may still suffer this imprisonment, still carry their chains.

Even persons who have known a deep and satisfying human love are affected. They have the advantage that they know something of what love has to offer, and do not feel that it has passed them by. But from this experience they are able to discern that there is a deeper, subtler, more penetrating love that is of God alone. The best and tenderest of human love calls of its nature to be pervaded with the goodness and permanence that God alone can give.

Hence the first area in which the Spirit will make Himself felt is the area of love. The waters that are poured out on the dried up earth will cause what is shrivelled up and apparently dead to live again; or if there be life, it will, as Christ promised, be given 'more abundantly'.*

* More will be found concerning Christian love in Weeks VI, Day 4 and VII Day 5.

2. Love flows into a second area, which may be called healing. For the deprivation of love has been a deep wound, and this begins to heal. And if there are other wounds, this same love of the Spirit will bind them up and heal them. For how could love do otherwise than heal? This is the order in which the Spirit proceeds. The healing can be of various kinds. It can take place in the moral order, which is always necessary; in the psychological order, which is frequently necessary, for those who are in misery cannot easily praise and thank the Lord. Finally it may occur in the physical order – but here the relationship between suffering and salvation in a given human life is not patent to us. Physical healings occur, for the power of the Spirit is total, but they do not occur with the same frequency as the inner healings. And this is not because the inner healings are less extraordinary, but because they are more essential. It would be a great mistake to underestimate the 'minor' healings which are almost of the essence of the release of the Spirit. They are only minor in the sense that they are not externally startling.

3. The third effect of the Spirit is that of conferring power. This is seen clearly enough in the ministerial gifts that have been described, but it should not (absolutely not!) be thought of as circumscribed by these gifts. For the power of the Spirit is like that of the sun – He gives life, joy, growth, vitality to all. He confers something of Himself to all who surrender to Him. It may be a new power in prayer, a new ability to sing the praises of the Lord, a new power to help him. But some kind of power it is. It is rooted in love, and liberated by the healing of those inner defects which before had such a constricting effect on a person, that the power of God could not operate freely in him – now it can.

St Luke seems to insist particularly that the conferring of the power of Christ on believers was in itself an effective witness to the Gospel truth, and that, time and time again, the people were moved by what had happened and so prepared to listen to the spoken word. Thus at the conclusion of the story relating how the lame man sitting at the Beautiful Gate of the Temple was healed [2] he observes 'All the people were giving glory to God for what had happened'[3]. It was the exhibition of divine power, heightened no doubt by the witness of the healed man who followed the apostles 'walking and jumping and praising God' that really set a challenge. Some praised God, others considered how to defend themselves[4]. Similar emphasis on the effect of divine power made manifest is found in *Acts.*[3] See also *Mark* 16: 17-18, which assumes that divine power accompanies the Gospel, and that this is a mark of those who spread the Gospel.

Day 5: The seven gifts of traditional theology

And the spirit of the Lord shall rest on him, the spirit of wisdom and of understanding; the spirit of counsel and fortitude; the spirit of knowledge and of godliness. And he shall be filled with the spirit of the fear of the Lord.

Is 11, 2, 3 (Douay)

This is the traditional* list of the Seven Gifts of the Holy Spirit referred to in the liturgical hymns (*Tu septiformis munere*) and mentioned in our catechisms down to this day. In fact the Hebrew text does not support the number seven; it only refers to six gifts; the seventh is mentioned in the Septuagint version.

We cannot, then, base a study of the gifts of the Spirit on an examination of this text. But it may be considered as significant in so far as it points to an area of the spiritual life about which we need to be aware; and also because so many theologians in every age have based their approach to the work of the Holy Spirit on this enumeration*. If modern scholarship shows that the text is but a shaky basis for what has been drawn from it, it is certain that the massive body of writing which came from meditation on

---

* The tradition is a very old one: thus St Ambrose instructs those who have been baptised: 'Remember that you have received the seal of the Spirit, the Spirit of wisdom and understanding, the Spirit of counsel and might, the Spirit of knowledge and godliness, the Spirit of holy fear, and preserve what you have received.'

it has its own insights, and is not to be passed by simply because scriptural scholarship was less advanced in those days. It is recognised that the inspirations of the Holy Spirit run strongly through the writings of the Fathers of the Church.

It is not then the enumeration that is important, nor the number seven, but the effect of the Spirit of the Lord when it 'rests' on a man.

The Spirit is always at work though we are not always willing to pay attention to Him. Our part is to be attentive. There are indeed many decisions in which to the best of our ability we think things out in a rational and religious way and then proceed to act on our conclusions. In this procedure the Spirit of God co-operates, for He cannot be absent from any part of Christian living. But there are also impulses and inspirations of the Spirit, and these will become more frequent and more pronounced as our will becomes more united with the will of God. In such cases we obey what we feel to be the inspiration of the Spirit. Individual cases in which the Holy Spirit is said to have given instruction abound in the *Acts of the Apostles*; but, without receiving instructions as clear as these, many persons are conscious of receiving inspiration from time to time; it is something beyond their own reasoning, or stronger than their own will-power.

If these impulses and inspirations are frequent, and if a person corresponds to them with full docility, then we may think of them as permanent in the soul. They are not permanent in the sense of a static quality, or as the standard of a man's intelligence is permanent; but the action of the Spirit is continuous, and the person lives with this consciousness. In these circumstances we may speak of him as having received such gifts of the Spirit.

An examination of the above list shows that they concern these areas of our personality – the intelligence, the will and the attitudes of piety and fear of the Lord. Full scale studies of each gift have been made, but here let us be contented to note how the Apostles were affected by the invasion of the Holy Spirit.

Firstly, as to their intelligence of divine things. Of what a different order is their understanding of these things as compared with that possessed by the writers of the Old Testament! There is an immense leap forward, not accounted for entirely by the teaching of Jesus while He was man, for the New Testament all too faithfully shows them as reacting with 'Old Testament' expectations – until the coming of the Spirit.

Secondly, the area of the will. What stands out more clearly than the new found fortitude of Peter after the day of Pentecost? This was truly a gift of the Spirit fortifying his will. And the same is seen in the other Apostles when they were brought before the Sanhedrin.

The word 'piety' – which sounds so dull in English – was for them an ever joyful communion with the living God. Those of them who wrote, and we can only suppose that the others were similar, left the impress of this joyful prayerfulness on their writings. The 'fear of the Lord' is a consequence of having experience at once of His transcendent majesty and infinite goodness. It is in no sense repellent, but indicates the profound consciousness of the creature in the presence of his Creator.

What then our text tells us is that we must learn to commit ourselves more and more to the guidance of the Spirit. We could not fall into the fallacy of expecting Him to take the place of our natural intelligence and supply us with will power; and some have fallen into this error. Avoiding this pitfall, we have to be ever more attentive and more docile, and the inspirations of the Holy Spirit will become more frequent in us. We shall, in theological language, be endowed with His gifts. It is another aspect of becoming rich in Christ.

Day 6: Prayer and joy

Be always joyful; pray continually; give thanks whatever happens; for this is what God in Christ wills for you.

I Thess 5: 16-18

These crisp and apparently straightforward counsels of St Paul lie outside the range of our natural possibilities. We cannot be *always* joyful. We are normally joyful when good things befall us, not otherwise; some people end up never joyful. Neither can we pray continually by simply deciding to do so. Continuous prayer supposes a heart that is ever homing in on God, and that is not in our power to command. Least of all do we find it possible to give thanks for whatever happens; we thank God for what we recognise as good and (at best) bow our heads in submission, perplexed endurance perhaps, when things go badly for us. If, under Christian instruction, we understand that 'whatever happens . . . is what God in Christ wills for you', when it is painful and unexpected we accept with fortitude and resignation, but find the giving true thanks beyond our power.

This is not to say that Christians do not cope valiantly with these teachings. Nor yet again that God does not come to meet them in their problems and their pain, as in their joys and triumphs. For this is the Christian way of life under all circumstances, and God's mercy is not circumscribed.

Our theme this week is 'richness in Christ', and it is one aspect of that richness that these apparently hard ascents are suddenly levelled out and made part of our lives, ordinary folk that we are. It is the result of receiving the release of the Spirit that the receiver knows joy which does not depend on earthly circumstances, prays more constantly because he is more conscious of thirst and more conscious that Christ fulfils His promise to give us to drink, and gives thanks for all things because the Holy Spirit teaches and prompts him to do so.

All these things are part of an enriched quality of prayer. For too many of us our prayer is essentially a matter of petition; we are kept on the right lines by our use of the Lord's prayer, by a few other prayers and the sacraments of the Church. We are ourselves most when we are asking for something, and very much ourselves if we feel disappointed because the petition does not seem to be granted; we wonder in the end if it ever reached its destination.

Our prayer should grow richer than that. Let it contain and begin with praise and thanksgiving. Hallowed, sanctified, blessed and praised be Thy name! And this when the Spirit is at work in us arises as a need, something we must do, without which life would be aimless and disorientated. We become aware that God is to be praised and thanked for first drawing us out of nothingness to have existence, which existence is the basis of happiness. We become aware that He called us again through the waters of baptism, and again through the other sacraments, that He holds us in His hand until He takes us to Himself in eternal joy. We become aware of His workings in others, whom He has created and loves and draws to Himself; we become concerned at resistance to His plans, we become aware that our part is to pray for their realisation, and know that this realisation is somehow incorporated in the fulfilment of the divine plan. We find ourselves praying that His will be done, knowing that this really is the ultimate in goodness and happiness, though we do not understand how; we do not understand how, but joy comes to the rescue, indicating that such always is the nature of God's loving plans for us and for all. Thus, through this new outpouring of the Spirit, we progress more rapidly into the dimension in which our prayer leads us to be praising God always, thanking Him with joy always for 'His will in Christ for us'. It is made possible for us to do what of our own nature we could not have done however hard we tried. And since this is a dimension of happiness, we come to pray always, as we can, however we can, conscious that these are the riches which are 'in Christ Jesus'.

Day 7: The importance of community

So you are no longer aliens or foreign visitors; you are citizens like all the saints, and part of God's household. You are a part of the building that has the apostles and prophets for its foundations, and Christ Jesus Himself for its main cornerstone. As every structure is aligned on Him, all grow into one holy temple in the Lord, and you too, in Him, are being built into a house where God lives, in the Spirit.

Eph 2: 19–22

While the 'release of the Spirit' in us does not actually confer spiritual maturity, it is undoubtedly a great help towards it; for without being fully 'alive' we shall mature with difficulty, and into rather a shrunken kind of maturity at that. The 'release,' then, is to speed us on our way and remove the barriers inside that impede spiritual growth.

God's plan of salvation is personal but also it is corporate: He saves us through the corporation that is His Body. Many gifts are for use in common and that implies a community of persons. Equally virtues are employed in community

The community can then be the instrument through which we mature spiritually. Many virtues are called forth by community living; unselfishness, sympathy, self-sacrifice, humility, generosity, etc. Life in community shows up lack of maturity and exposes imaginary virtues. In community we have the chance to share our virtues, help one another with our burdens, and be loving with one another in our weaknesses.

There is of course more than one kind of community. There is the parish, the religious community, the lay institute, maybe the charismatic collectivity within the parish. Each has its possibilities. So strongly is the need felt today for community as an aid to spiritual life that all over the world there are settlements, enterprises, undertakings, where people are drawn together by a spiritual bond. They recognise – although this may have nothing to do with a specifically charismatic movement – the need for spiritual help and understanding, and the bond of love in human society. They testify all too eloquently to the fact that such a bond has perished almost completely from the normal units of our modern society.

Every Christian needs community to practise the fulness of his Christian life. The charismatic is no exception: indeed in this (as in other matters) he feels the inner force of the apostolic teaching and will want to be part of a community which the Holy Spirit keeps fully alive. Ideally this is a normal social grouping – a religious house or a settlement or a parish – but circumstances will frequently be such that the members of a charismatic group are a fragment of a larger unity in which they are seen as 'something special'; perhaps approved of or perhaps tolerated.

Whatever his position, the charismatic is called to give to his community to the full extent of his power. He has to realise in his own life and bear witness to the fact that the community is a household built of God; as the Apostle says, its corner-stone is Christ Jesus, on whom are laid the Apostles and prophets; and then their successors, even unto our own time. He knows that he has to contribute to this, and it is by so doing that he grows in maturity of spiritual life. Sometimes the very rules of community life or the differences and awkwardnesses that occur between human persons are the occasion of this growth. How will he practise humility, unless there is someone to submit to? How will he exercise charity unless to the other members of Christ's household? How can he speak of growing in the fruit of the Spirit — of gentleness, patience, kindness, self-control — if there is nobody around on whom to exercise these qualities?

And if giving is asked for, there is also receiving. For at a charismatic meeting those gathered together in Christ's name bring down by their united prayer the gifts of the Spirit and the divine response to their most human needs. There too certain gifts such as that of healing or prophecy often emerge and develop. It is there also that something beyond individual blessings often emerges: the capacity to show forth what the body of Christ should really be, to show forth, that is, Christ Himself living, not physically, but really and mystically and with power in the congregation of His followers.

It is then essential that, both to be sustained and to be fully faithful one must belong to a community, a Christian grouping of some sort. One's basic helpfulness to the group will not lie in ministerial gifts, but in that other list of spiritual fruit 'love, joy, peace, patience . . .' which will include humility. Indeed humility is the surest sign of all that the Spirit is at work. Mary, the mother of Jesus, knew this when she lifted up her voice and sang:

My soul glorifies the Lord,
My spirit rejoices in God, my Saviour,
He looks on His servant *in her lowliness* . . .[1]

Lowliness, joy, the praise of God, these are the first gifts which the charismatic must try to bring to the community.

Week five: Some impediments

In the previous weeks we have followed this trail: Firstly we considered the Divine Invitation as made in Scripture and how this corresponds to our deepest need which is for salvation. In our third week we developed the concept of how this salvation is wrought in us through the bringing of *new life* to our natural man, and the implications for those who have already received baptism and confirmation. Last week was concerned with the wonderful effects of the release of the Spirit within us – the *riches* that should be ours. But there may yet be *barriers* to our reception of this release; barriers that may prevent us seeking it or barriers that may impede its results. These will be treated in this fifth week. Not all will concern any one reader; possibly he may not feel concerned by any – but most of us will have some impediments clogging up the free flowing of the Spirit in our lives. He removes them, but we co-operate by examining and understanding them. And therefore it will be useful to have a look at some of these common impediments to our freedom.

The reader who has worked through these spiritual exercises over the past four weeks, has the information to seek for himself the release of the Spirit. But information is not enough. Other signs of being ready are as important.

These are principally:

1. The desire to install Christ in one's life as true Lord, a desire expressed for the first time or as a deepened renewal, according to our history. The desire to invite Him to take the driving seat; and the desire to move over, so as to let Him do so.

2. Correspondingly, a decision that with the help of Our Lord, one will turn against sin, and all forms of wrong-doing, and all sentiments in oneself that may displease Him.

3. Concomitantly with these desire-decisions an awareness that one can fulfil nothing alone; and a desire that the Lord may complete in us what He has begun, and bring these stirrings to that fulfilment which He alone can work in us.

When these sentiments are present the road is clear, and we will be well advised to contact some one able to help and direct us personally towards receiving the release of the Spirit.

Where these sentiments are not present, then apparently the time is not yet. Either way it will be useful to continue in prayer, and the consideration of some possible barriers may be found useful.

Here are certain prayers you may say frequently. They are short, as this makes it easier to repeat them. If you find that you can make short prayers of your own, do not hesitate to make use of them instead of those you read here.

Lord, complete in me what you have begun. Make me so turn to you, that you can turn to me, you who love me more than I can grasp. Lord, grant me to love you truly.

Lord, grant me to recognise in myself whatever may be a barrier separating me from you; grant me the strength to remove it totally.

Act of Faith: Lord, I believe in your power to change me, and in your love to do so. I believe that you are drawing me to yourself and I wish to respond.

Act of Praise and Thanksgiving: Lord, I thank and praise you for all the blessings you grant me. Lord, increase my power to praise and thank you.

Act of Petition: Grant me, Lord, to be renewed in the Spirit. Grant me those gifts which will enable me to sing your praises, to pray to you as I ought, to help and heal your suffering members.

Day 1: Doubts and fears

Simon Peter said, 'Lord, where are you going? Why can't I follow You?'

John 13: 36

Thomas said, 'Lord, we do not know where You are going, so how can we know the way?'

John 14: 5

Philip said, 'Lord, let us see the Father, and then we shall be satisfied.'

John 14: 8

Judas (this was not Judas Iscariot) said to Him, 'Lord what is all this about?'

John 14: 22

The disciples had lived happily with Christ, wondered at the beauty of His teaching, gasped in admiration at His miracles, occasionally worked miracles themselves, known themselves to be especially chosen, and looked forward to still better things to come, when the Kingdom should be set up, and their personal thrones assigned to them. Consequently they were disturbed and dismayed at the tone of our Lord's discourse after the Last Supper. This talk of going away, of sending another one in his place, of being seen in the world no more, of returning to the Father — none of it fitted with their expectations. It was a new dimension to his teaching, and their reaction was one of anxiousness and fear. They preferred things as they were.

It is not unnatural if many of us react somewhat doubtfully to talk of a new dimension in spiritual life, and one which is to differ markedly from what has gone before. The sinner will feel: This is not for me; this is outside my type of life altogether. The practising Christian may think: But I already have all that the Church offers and teaches by her normal means. Why should I be led up this new path? Is it necessary? Is it even safe? They will be reacting like the Apostles, who had already benefited from so much of Christ's teaching, yet had one or two experiences to come that would shatter them first and transform them later.

The two hindrances to this newness of life are a sinful life and unwillingness (even in a good person) to accept it, perhaps through distrust. Thus it is possible that a reader who has persevered thus far, and is still interested, but dubious, will be a prey to indecision and uncertainty.

Certain things can hold us back. Piety, whatever our form of it may be, is normally conservative. We hold on to what we have. Our Lord knew this: 'People do not put new wine into old wineskins; if they do the skins burst, the wine runs out and the skins are lost. No, they put new wine into fresh skins and both are preserved.'[1] He meant that the Mosaic law could not swell to serve as the vessel of his doctrine; he needed a new kingdom altogether. Now Christ's doctrine is always new, always fermenting, but it does not follow that the way we have grasped it, the particular practices which make up our translation of the Gospel into our personal lives are equally capable of growth. We tend to personal fixation, and hence to fear, and resent anything that suggests 'newness'. Yet 'newness' within orthodoxy is of the very essence of life. A devout person often has a fixed idea of the nature of the work that the Holy Spirit should perform in his soul. He is not conscious of the fixation, or probably not, but it is there all the same. And the Holy Spirit may not be able to operate with freedom within such limits. St Benedict provided that his monks should at the beginning of their Divine Office daily recite the words: Today, if ye shall hear His voice, harden not your hearts.[2]

Fear and suspicion, then, motivated by a perfectly human conservatism, even a sense of self-conservation, may make it difficult for some to yield themselves in a new commitment to Christ. If they could but grasp that He, the Lord, issues to them a new invitation, corresponding to a fresh outbreak of his generosity, then this difficulty dissolves. He has been with them on their way so far – but now He has a fresh sending of the Spirit to offer them. Such fears should be seen in this light; it is a question of confidence in Him.

Another obstacle, submerged but very real, could be the idea that to 'go charismatic' is not really quite respectable. Prayer, yes; but speaking in tongues, no! Lord spare me that! I do not need any fresh tongues — and what will people say of me? Certainly Nicodemus the devout and respectable Pharisee had problems about seeking out Jesus that did not occur to Bartimaeus, hollering his head off by the road side. Nor did the young man, rich, devout, well-brought up, find it easier to join the ranks of the followers of Jesus than the ex-harlot who anointed his feet in a sudden outburst of love and repentance. Yes, we should count fear of seeming odd, a bit crazy, or at any rate of being thought of as ill-balanced among the deterrents that cause unwillingness to get involved. St Teresa in a devastating passage[3] points to a hidden holding on to respectability as a reason why many devout persons decline God's favours.

These are individual fears. Ironically other fears may be based on danger to the community — whether it be parish or religious community or other grouping. There may be a fear: will not this movement lead to division among us? Is it not divisive if part of the community speak in tongues (and interpret them too!) and the other half are left outside the magic circle? And worse still, if the charismatics have an air of superiority about them.

There is perhaps some confusion here as to whether the fear is a fear of the action of the Holy Spirit or a fear of the reaction of human beings to Him or even a fear of a 'new style' in prayer which appeals to some but not to others.

The complete answers to such fears and to similar ones cannot be developed fully here — the simple answer is: examine more carefully the make-up of your particular fear. The following brief points may help.

1. When the whole body desires the gift of the Spirit nobody will be left out. And this is how a body of Christians should be.

2. Certainly the gifts received will be different to different groups and people — not all will be the phenomenal or apparently sensational type. This is not the essence of the gifts of the Spirit. The great gift is the Holy Spirit uniting all in a supernatural sympathy, compassion and love, and in an awareness that they are led to this by the Spirit of God.

3. Gifts vary according to position and need. The increase of spiritual capacity which the Holy Spirit may bring to a person in authority, say a parish priest or a religious superior, is far more important for them than say the gift of tongues.

4. The Body of Christ should be rich in every gift⁴; otherwise it is poorer than it should be. The gifts are complementary, they build up the body. If they are found to be divisive, that must be attributed to misuse or misunderstanding. The alternative to mis-using spiritual gifts is not to avoid them altogether.

Finally, a point for religious communities which naturally enough have their fears, often based on ignorance. Consider: if the Holy Spirit is visibly at work among you, are you likely to suffer from a lack of vocations?

Day 2: Sinfulness

When self-indulgence is at work, the results are obvious; fornication, gross indecency and sexual irresponsibility; idolatry, sorcery; feuds, wrangling, jealousy, bad temper and quarrels; disagreements, factions, envy; drunkenness, orgies and similar things. I warn you now as I warned you before; those who behave like this will not inherit the Kingdom of God.

Gal 5:20, 21

A similar list of vices and a similar warning was addressed to the Corinthians ¹ – which mentions also sexual perverts, thieves, swindlers . . .

Perhaps the first thing that these down-to-earth warnings should bring home to us is that Christians were being called from the ranks of sinful people, of unacceptable people and criminal people. Even such as these were not outside the call of the Gospel. And neither are they outside it today. For Christ's invitation is truly universal, and He became notorious Himself for eating and drinking with sinners. No one then should say to himself 'I am outside the range of salvation'.

On the other hand St Paul makes it equally clear that when such a one is called and answers the call, he has to leave his vices behind him. No one is beyond receiving the call; but the call is to

88

repentance. One might well infer from these texts that St Paul's converts were in fact having quite a struggle to get rid of their former habits. Indeed, in the first *Letter to the Corinthians* it is clear that they were not altogether successful; that there were moral battles still to be won. The extremely important lesson here is:

1. No condition, however sinful, is outside the range of Christ's call.

2. Sinful actions and thoughts are incompatible with the Christian life. They are, each and every one of them a barrier to the life in the Spirit.

3. The Holy Spirit is stronger than these things — even if we are not — and can overcome them in us.

They are rooted in self-indulgence; that is the first point to grasp. And they are its bitter fruits. But very often even self-indulgence is an attempt to get something out of life; some enjoyment, some value, something that satisfies; and without some joy, some value, something that satisfies, how shall we live? How shall the sinner escape from his sin, if it is the plank on which he swims, or seems to float, above the shifting and unsustaining circumstances of his life? When St Augustine of Hippo was approaching conversion, he tells us that the pleasures of the flesh called out to him, 'Can you live without us?'; though he adds: 'They did so very faintly now.'

The essence of the matter is really this: we cannot live without some satisfaction. And we seek, even if we do not find, the fullest satisfaction available. It does require, then, a real act of faith for the sinner to turn his back on his sins; they are so much a part of him. But it is essential for him to realise that he is not being asked to walk out into a bleak land called 'Holiness', but invited to come into the warmth.

For the Holy Spirit knows and will supply the answer to those needs which a sinner has known how to satisfy only with fruits of bitterness.

For lust, and whatever satisfaction it can bring, the Holy Spirit will put love in his heart. The difficulty is to believe it!

For drunkenness (or drugs — an equivalent type of dependence) the Spirit will give him to drink of the divine waters, and restore his independence. The difficulty is to believe it!

For bad temper, quarrelsomeness etc, the Spirit knows the remedy, for He touches deep down in the heart, where the trouble really starts. The difficulty is to believe it!

For envy and jealousy, the remedy is very simple; the sinner becomes aware that he is rich in a new way. He is more anxious now to share than he was before to claim. The difficulty is make oneself open for the enrichment.

The barrier of sin has then to be surmounted, or pulled down. It is written: 'With my God I leap the rampart'[2] And this power may be effected by the release of the Spirit. But more than that, since, as has been said, a man cannot live without happily the joy of realised values, this too shall be supplied him on the other side of the rampart; and with these, strength to overcome what before held him in chains. He will utter his prayer with the psalmist:

> This God who girds me with strength
> And makes my way without blame.[3]

This does not mean that there will be no battles, but that the weapons of victory, which are joy and love and prayer, are available and may be grasped by those who will seek them.

Day 3: Depression

You have plunged me to the bottom of the pit,
to its darkest, deepest place,
weighted down by Your anger
drowned beneath Your waves.

Ps 88: 6, 7

If sin in its innumerable forms is the great barrier to the entry to the Kindom of Heaven, there are other barriers which may, at any rate on this earth, prevent us from feeling ourselves true citizens of the Kingdom. Very widespread today is that burden we call depression. The depressed person will often feel that he has 'lost his faith'. What good is it to him? It brings him no happiness; it casts no sunshine on his existence. The theological books, the Scriptures themselves may proclaim the great benefits that God has lavished on mankind – it makes no difference: the depressed person is thoroughly miserable and incapable of interest in anything. Nor can he pray – least he does not feel he can pray – or that the skies lighten if he does. With his depression goes inevitably isolation; for others have to be on their way, they cannot sit in silent gloom beside him; would it help if they did? So he feels isolated from man and that God is either 'useless' or indifferent. This depression is then really an extension of the kingdom of darkness, a great evil. But Christ came to overcome all forms of evil, and primarily those that afflict our souls.

Depression is not to be identified with sorrow. For Christ knew sorrow and frustration to an extreme degree. He wept over Jerusalem, bewailing His failure to convert her and foreseeing her fate. He was saddened by many things. He was 'a man of sorrows and familiar with suffering'.[1] But he was not a depressed person; on the contrary He invited 'all you who labour and are overburdened' to come to Him, saying 'I will give you rest'.[2]

And this He does when He sends his Spirit into the weary breast, bringing its harvest of 'love, joy, peace, patience . . .'[3] just that enrichment of which the depressed person is deprived, and with it the power to form human relationships, to render service, to take an interest in the good things that life offers.

The problem of the depressed person is often just how to break out of the imprisoning circle. He cannot follow advice, for he has no strength to do so; he cannot pray, or thinks he cannot pray – for what is the use? he is unrelieved by hearing promises, even God's promises, for there is a gulf set between him and such hopes, and no apparent way across. How is such an impasse to be solved?

Firstly, nothing is here so opportune as the helping hand of friends who are acquainted with the ways of the Spirit. The sufferer, having no strength in his own faith may have to lean heavily on the faith of others. They will not cease to pray for him, and as best they can introduce him gently to the reality of the Good News as they have themselves found it. Jesus worked many wonders at the instance of the friends of sick people. A notable example is that of the paralytic, brought by his friends to the house at Capernaum; for we read that Jesus 'seeing their faith' cured the man they had taken so much trouble to bring to him.[4]

Secondly, if there is a definite neurosis, psychiatry is not to be regarded as unchristian or as an alternative to the work of the Spirit. God is the author of all kinds of healing, whether through the skill of doctors or otherwise. Doctors learn to use the laws that God has implanted in human nature, or the healing quality to be found in natural objects, for our healing. Whether psychiatry or some other branch of medicine can be of help or not, is a separate question to be decided on its own merits. To employ it does not imply lack of faith in the power of the Holy Spirit; nor does the invocation of the Holy Spirit imply a repudiation of psychiatry or medicine. But it remains true that the Holy Spirit can if He chooses do the healing work Himself, and He has two things to do which psychiatry cannot do. For psychiatry cannot supply the orientation and the values that can give meaning to a human life: these are of God. Neither can psychiatry actually supply the 'love, joy, peace, patience, benignity . . .' which are the wholeness of a human being, as they are also his holiness. It can normalise the soil in which these seeds are to grow. It can clear away twisted growths that encumber the soil, and may be useful for this.

It remains that depressed people, should recall that in fact we are not spiritually alone. How depressed was the psalmist when he uttered the words quoted above! But we must try to elicit a desire, a spark, a hope, a turning, towards Him who can bring us comfort.

If you can make the effort to praise and thank God for all things — including present sadness — He will know how to lead you out of the valley of darkness. For it is not His will that you should be separated from Him by depression. Give Him thanks, then, that He has joy in store for you.

Day 4: Failure to forgive

And forgive us our debts
As we forgive those who are in debt to us.

Mt 6: 12

Sin is a barrier, obviously so. Depression can in fact also prove to be another. Now let us turn to a third barrier, which is a very real one, and can, alas! be found in the hearts of quite 'righteous' people. It can be the root problem of somebody who calls on God – and yet seems to do so in vain. He wonders why.

This barrier is the failure to forgive others. Usually, though not necessarily, they will be persons who either are or have been near to us; for in fact such persons have greater power to do us harm, even unwittingly. Thus some people who have suffered from a character defect in their parents, do not forgive them. Or it may be a situation between husband and wife. Or the situation that can arise between a religious and his or her superior. The situation may long have passed away – the person causing the embitterment may be dead – but the sense of injury remains, and there is no forgiveness.

Sometimes these things can have small beginnings; a mere minor misunderstanding leads to a sense of resentment, and this small wound instead of healing becomes inflamed. 'Resentment is found in the heart of fools' says *Ecclesiastes*,[1] and this is true, for the person harbouring resentment will be the main sufferer from it, since it distorts the whole soul. But then are we not all fools, more or less, clamouring for our 'justice' and to be properly appreciated? and hurt when this does not happen? And how thin a line there is between being 'hurt', which is no sin, and being resentful, which is going to be the breeding ground of many sins!

However, everyone suffers injury somewhere along the line, great or small. Hence we are all likely to suffer from resentment, and many there are whose wounds, caused by this, have become inflamed beyond the ordinary means of healing.

That is why Our Lord teaches us to pray 'Forgive us our debts as we forgive those who are in debt to us.' It is the only petition with a condition attached to it – 'as we forgive'. And in case we should overlook this connection, Our Lord went back to the subject after the prayer, to explain: Yes, if you forgive others their failings, your heavenly Father will forgive you yours; but if you do not forgive others, your Father will not forgive your failings either.[2]

Nothing could be plainer than that. And yet Our Lord makes his will clearer still; one of his longest parables – that of the servant who owed his master ten thousand talents, and was owed one hundred pence – is devoted to the same theme.[3] This parable does make His point of view abundantly clear. He finds it intolerable that we should turn to Him for the forgiveness of so many sins and so much sinfulness, and yet refuse our forgiveness to some 'fellow-servant' who has injured us.

It is true that for some of us this remains very difficult. We look back: 'He (She) ruined my life. I cannot forgive him.' 'If only he were punished as he deserves then I could forgive, but not while he prospers, and I suffer because of him.' 'If only he would ask me to forgive him . . . but he doesn't care!' And so on. It can be very difficult: we have our measure of justice, and would apparently suffer anything for the satisfaction of seeing it fulfilled. Divine justice interests us less, largely because we are less aware of the state of our indebtedness.

We have, then, to make every effort to overcome ourselves, using every motive that Our Lord sets before us. And we cannot dodge the issue. Perhaps, if we are unable to reach full forgiveness, we can reach a desire-decision, that is to say we really want to do what we don't actually succeed in doing, but we sincerely desire, and this is in effect the decision of our will; but we have to wait on grace for the fuller healing of our wound, for we cannot do it ourselves. In this state we can indeed present ourselves before God, for our will is to do His will, our desire is to fulfil His command; only strength is lacking. If we can reach this point sincerely, grace will be accorded to our weakness and we shall progress. It may even be that we have enough of the spirit of forgiveness to ask for the release of the Spirit in us, and then the effect will be that we are given more.

Sometimes people ask for the release of the Spirit, and apparently it does not happen. This may be an invitation to examine themselves anew to see if there are hidden resentments, un-forgiving sentiments, harsh judgements, which have to be turned out of their hiding places and rejected. And then the Spirit will make his presence felt, when the word of the Lord has been fulfilled. We have had to find out and forgive what had been covered up, but nevertheless unforgiven. So the way is made open to the Spirit, who can now flood the soul.

Day 5: Our wrong attitude to God's Fatherhood

While he was still a long way off his father was moved with pity. He ran to the boy, clasped him in his arms and kissed him tenderly.
Lk 15: 21

Thus in the parable of the 'prodigal' son, the Gospel shows the father as scanning the roads in the hope of getting a glimpse of a returning wanderer, and then, unable to wait or even to walk at a sober pace, running down the road to meet him, to embrace him and kiss him tenderly. He does not wait for apologies or ex-planations. 'You are my son and I love you' is his whole speech. Surely that was fatherly love indeed!

Now the object of asking the Holy Spirit to come and take possession of us is that we may enter more fully into the Kingdom of God our Father, and may know that Father in all His goodness.

For some there may be here a barrier, conscious or un-conscious, in the psychological fact that they have never had a warm relationship with their human father. For it is from our human father that we get indelible ideas of what fatherhood is about – at any rate for us. And so, if that relationship was a failure, or has had a traumatic effect, a person will receive words about God our Father in terms of what he knows. Or again, such a one will hear these things with eager ears, feeling a need for a true father the more because he has not known that joy before – and yet with a lingering doubt that this can really be part of the pattern of his life. In Our Lord's time and country the relationship between child and father was intimate, and Our Lord assumes this when He teaches us about God our Father. But in our time and age, the word 'Father' unfortunately may not bring to some the associations that Our Lord surrounds it with. That is why the words quoted above need special attention, not least by those of us who may be slow to recognise the loving quality of God's fatherhood, for want of having experienced the human pattern which should have prepared the way for it. And perhaps in our modern civilisation they are not few.

Another barrier that can stand between quite righteous people and God their Father is that deep down they don't want to be interfered with. They have thrown off paternalism and don't appreciate the subject being raised again. They will serve God, yes, recognise His laws, yes, but they do not really trust Him enough to submit their lives unreservedly to His guidance. No doubt that was why He sent His only Son 'in the form of a slave' to be one of us, to encourage us, as one of us, to really trust the Father . . . unto the end. We do well to examine our feelings. Do we hope for much from our Heavenly Father here and now (not only in another world)? Or do we feel that what comes from Him will take the form of law-giving, judgement – conceivably approval, quite likely punishment? Do we feel that He is, characteristically, punishing us now? Or can we say that we see Him as one who has abandoned his watchtower, and is already running down the road to embrace us and kiss us? though we certainly are arriving without any accumulation of riches, but rather in rags and tatters. For that is what Christ here teaches us. And if we have a fear-psychology about Him, the notion that He has exacting standards rather than the feeling that He wants to put his arms round us and embrace us, then let us strive to adjust our focus by examining anew Christ's teaching. The Holy Spirit will come to our aid, but we do well to aware of any defect in our psychological make-up which might cause us to sheer away from the encounter.

There are perhaps two types of persons who may have the

greatest difficulty in seeking the release of the Spirit. There are those who feel that they are hypocrites; who are aware of a vast gap between the person they are supposed to be and the person they are. The gap may be made by real sins of which they, but no one else is aware. What are God's conditions before He receives them? Is not the cost of a change of direction intolerable to them? And there are those who more or less consciously have, over the years, deliberately built up a wall of hardness of heart. They have in their own sense 'overcome the world'; now they are imprisoned behind a wall they cannot demolish. To them also the prospect of a change of heart appears an impossibility.

Well, the Heavenly Father is running down the road; at least allow Him to put his arms round you and embrace you. Do not deny Him His joy. When He has done that you can sort things out together afterwards. But first just allow Him to claim you as His child, and be willing to let Him show you this love. Need you be afraid of that? For fear is a large part of the trouble.

Day 6: Self-love

This people honours me only with lip-service, while their hearts are far from me.

Mk 7: 6 (Is 29: 13)

A barrier to the realisation of God's plans for us that may exist is that our habitual, if unconscious motivation is self-love. Now we are in fact so made that we are bound to love ourselves. In the Old Testament it was written 'thou shalt love thy neighbour as thyself', and nobody doubted that one loved oneself unto death. This is a law of our being which we cannot escape, and when our Lord heard these words quoted by a scribe he fully approved the answer. But there is another law imprinted equally profoundly in our being — it is the first law of all. As creatures we are made to

97

love the Lord our God with all our soul and with all our strength – and this is the only way in which we shall ever reach fulfilment. When we speak of the defect of self love, then, we do not refer to either of these laws by which we seek fulfilment for our deepest needs, even as the flower opens its bud and turns towards the life-giving sun. To seek the fulfilment for which we are made, body and soul, is right, proper and inevitable; our fulfilment is to be full of God's glory, to be genuinely glorious creatures, perfectly in harmony with the loving design of our Creator.

If therefore we speak of self-love as a false motivation we mean that kind of self-determination which sets its own goal for our destiny, here and now, and then directs all thoughts, actions and loves to meet that small self-prescribed destiny. Persons who make no profession of religion will do this ruthlessly, and there must be an equally complete admission of their mistake before they can start co-operating with God in the fulfilment of their true destiny. But self-love is often far more subtle than that.

For many who are servants of God, there are whole areas of our personality withdrawn from any integration with the pursuit of our final end. Sometimes these may not be very difficult to recognise; but often in the very service of God itself, the same blindness is present. We speak in terms of doing God's will, perhaps believe that we are doing it, and yet are motivated by ambition, desire for reputation, for influence, for power, for the fulfilment of our human needs, and we remain unaware of this. Now there is always alloy in the service we would offer to God, until He takes it out, which He will do if we are aware of the need and ask Him to do so. This calls for a deep trust in Him, that He will make the necessary change in our motivation, and therefore in all our value-judgements. This, then, must be our guiding principle: true self-love recognises God's loving conception of what He wants us to be and do, and surrenders joyously to it; false self-love attempts to use God's powers, whether natural talents or Spirit-given gifts, for our own purposes, comfort or glory. It is of great importance that we seek the release of the Spirit in us, not for what we may be able 'to get out of it', but only that we may joyously allow God's plans to be developed in us.

Only one book in the Bible is written in what we could call a humorous vein. This is the prophecy of Jonah, in which the prophet is shown from start to finish as contending unsuccessfully and ridiculously with a patient God, whose plans he does not approve of. Jonah doesn't approve of Ninevites, nor of God's mercy towards them. The root cause of the dissension is that Jonah is always motivated by self-will and self-love; he is never aware of this. The results are disconcerting and ridiculous as God employs one instrument after another to cure him. Perhaps the sacred author wished to indicate that self-love is in fact a sad and ridiculous quality in any one called to serve the great God of heaven and earth, and to serve as an instrument in the fulfilment of His plans.

Pray then that God may give you ever increasing purity of heart, freedom from self-seeking, and a true understanding of how your love for yourself is to be caught up into His love for you.

Day 7: The wiles of Satan

He rebuked Peter and said to him: Get behind me, Satan! Because the way you think is not God's way, but men's.

Mk 8: 33

St Peter, on hearing our Lord's prophecy that He would be rejected and condemned to death, ventured to remonstrate with our Lord; it was a natural reaction from one who loved Christ, but our Lord nevertheless sternly reproved him, for trying to turn Him away from the accomplishment – painful as it would be – of His mission. We too have to grasp that Satan will be at work trying to turn us away from the accomplishment of God's designs in us.

This could well be something that happens to you, dear reader, even now. For you are approaching the reception of a great grace, and a definitive new commitment of your whole self to the following of Christ. It is then to be expected that Satan would want to interfere with this as best he can. Remember that our war individually is but the tiniest fragment of the war that goes on in the whole world between the powers of darkness and God's redeeming power. It is, and remains for us a mystery, but one that is palpable in its effects; and, as one of the human race, you are involved in it too. Hence it may well be expected that Satan is likely to try to confuse you and hinder you.

He may suggest doubts. You are not worthy to enter into such a life as is promised to you. You can't rise to it. . . .

Or: You are already well educated in Christian teaching, you are established in the Church of God. What need to take up anything fresh? It is enough to keep to your present practices of prayer and normal Christian habits.

Or: There is something suspicious about this new 'baptism'. Does not the conferring of grace depend simply on the frequent reception of the sacraments?

Or: Why should the Holy Spirit provide new graces in our time, just at this moment of the Church's history? (Why indeed!) In fact the Holy Spirit is always providing new graces according to the needs of each age. It is much less important to explain how He acts than to recognise his touch, to accept, to surrender.

There are many strategies that Satan can employ to confuse us, who are after all so inexperienced in a spiritual world which to us remains invisible. The commitment of faith is a commitment to an invisible God – yet it is a very real one, and will affect all our future. But we are on the brink of changing a tangible, familiar, realistic, 'normal' life style for an act of faith in an unseen God. Satan steps in, and suggests that it is all very unreal. Let us get back to common sense and put aside these strange invitations. . . . Yet do we not know how gladness follows the taking of a deeply right decision? Once it is done the fog clears away; we wonder that our eyesight was so poor before. Vigorously we need to say 'Get behind me Satan! I will go forward.'

Plenty of other subtle temptations can be suggested, and some not too subtle ones. One pitfall is to suppose that charismatics are some kind of spiritual 'hippy', whose notions of prayer or way of praying cannot possibly be suitable for us. If we think this we are far from the truth. It is indeed sometimes true that 'hippies' become charismatics, carrying something of their life-style with them, since there is great freedom in the prayer meetings. But the fact that some people embody their prayer in a 'cultural baggage' that is alien to us is unimportant and accidental, and need not concern us at all. Spiritual movements contain persons of all kinds, the crowd that surrounded the Saviour were a very mixed lot. In fact that was why some people objected to Him. A community will work out its own type of prayer-meeting according to its own needs. Likewise in a parish, those groups succeed whose style of prayer-meeting corresponds to the needs of the participants. Many would be surprised if they realised that among the participants in charismatic prayer meetings were persons who were shy, lonely, elderly, settled perhaps, in all the ways of an older generation . . . yet very much at home in an atmosphere where the work of the Spirit is to integrate all in one love.

Here is a prayer which may help at this stage. It is an act of confidence in God:

'The Lord is my shepherd:
I shall not want.
He maketh me to lie down in green pastures:
He leadeth me beside the still waters.
He restoreth my soul:
He leadeth me in the path of righteousness,
For His name's sake.
Yea, though I walk through the valley of the shadow of death,
I will fear no evil;
For Thou art with me
Thy rod and Thy staff they comfort me.'[7]

Week six: The ongoing process

Since the release of the Spirit within us enables us to turn to God with an undivided heart, it is a new beginning, a special grace which we must follow up by all means in our power. St Paul, after all the privileges and revelations that he had received, was deeply conscious of this ongoing process of growth in Christ. 'Forgetting' he said 'what lies behind me and reaching out for what lies ahead, I press towards the goal, to win the prize which is God's call to the life above, which is in Christ Jesus'.[1] This must be our task also; under the stirring of the Holy Spirit to form or deepen those habits of Christian virtue, which must be acquired or deepened as the case may be. If they are already formed the path will be easier and the Christian will know how to co-operate with the new gift he has received; if they are not, a struggle lies ahead, but one for which the Holy Spirit supplies strength. In the following pages attention is drawn to the Christian virtues – there are no new ones – and habits which make up the Christian's way of life.

Day 1: Taking up the Cross of Christ

He called the people and His disciples to Him and said: 'If anyone wants to be a follower of mine, let him renounce himself, and take up his cross, and follow me.

Mk 8: 34

Here we have one of Jesus' most significant sayings. It occurs in all three synoptic Gospels. Mark and Luke[1] in their corresponding passages seem to emphasise the publicity of this pronouncement. It is not just one of his sayings, but one which he calls disciples and the common people together to hear; it is basic. St Matthew[2] does not emphasise so much the publicity as the divisive quality of this announcement; he gives us Christ's warning that the standard He was setting would divide families; His was not the kind of teaching that, if fulfilled, would pass unnoticed. If the sending anew of the Spirit of the Saviour into our hearts brings with it the courage and joy to undertake a fuller commitment in His service, it will also give us to understand the significance of this saying also.

What after all do we understand by the expression 'Take up his cross and follow Me'? We should understand quite simply that a true following of Christ, a true commitment to Him, involves us in a certain amount of personal sacrifice, of self-denial and maybe of disapproval from the world in which we live. Let us take note of some of the things which form for us the cross of Christ.

Firstly, there has to be a definite turning away from sin and from all forms of wrong-doing; and, as our world is constituted, there are forms of wrong-doing which are licensed or tolerated simply because they are so common. But to turn away from all sin and wrong-doing is easier said than done. It may hurt. Wrongdoing of some kind may have been a source of steady satisfaction; to turn from it may seem like undertaking a life of constant tension. Our aim, then, should be so to surrender to our Saviour that He, in return, sending His Spirit, may give us the power to overcome these obstacles. Nevertheless it will remain that there is a struggle with bad habits, which, even if apparently annihilated, are likely to attack us anew later on. The first taking up the cross is, then, the renunciation of all and anything that may be pleasurable to our human nature, but which is recognised as unholy.

Secondly, the practice of virtue can be arduous. To be patient when I feel like it, yes; but always patient? That can be arduous indeed. And so with other virtues: to pray when the Spirit prompts can be easy enough; but what if the Spirit is not around today? One must still offer one's poor best (which may actually be more acceptable than we suspect — for it is an act of faith and fidelity). Likewise the charity of making ourselves available to others; it can call for putting aside what we had legitimately in mind to do for ourselves. The practice of chastity, too, can be an arduous battle. In binding ourselves to do these things unremittingly we follow Christ, and because for us sinners they are against the grain, we can say that they are a carrying of the cross.

Then there are trials which come to us in the carrying out of Christ's doctrine, trials inflicted by those who disapprove or deride or obstruct or take advantage. Christ threw down His challenge about these things when He said 'Happy those who are persecuted in the cause of right: theirs is the Kingdom of Heaven.'[3] These words are not merely a promise, nor a culmination; they are of the essence of carrying the cross of Christ. It is a way of life identified indeed with happiness and blessedness, but also marked by a separation from worldly means of advancement, from a dependence on those conditions which the world considers indispensable for the good life. The fully committed Christian will be like his Master, and like Him run into a headwind of the disapproval of the worldly.

But it is not impossible. There are those who, accepting the universality of the conflict between good and evil and seeing how the latter is identified with self-indulgence, seeing that their Master's life was humanly speaking one of poverty and abstinence even from such good things as married life, commit themselves also to lives of self-denial in these same matters. Their motive is that by sharing His self-denial, they may share also the freedom and universality of His love. And so 'with a mighty joy'[4] they offer all things that they have or might have and follow Him in lives of complete dedication. This is what the vows of religious are about.

These then are some of the things Christians understand when they ponder their Master's challenging words. The meaning of those words can be extended to cover any suffering which comes to the Christian from any source, seeking as he does to identify the actualities of his life with Christ's teachings.

No one, however, should conclude that Christ is a hard Master, laying a heavy burden of tribute on His own. He Himself declared the opposite, for 'My burden' he said 'is light.'[5] To find it so and yet to carry it fully, for this we need the strengthening of the Spirit of God. The Spirit will not come between us and the cross of Christ: He will heal us in ourselves and so strengthen us, and fill us with joy, so that we carry the cross after Christ with eager hearts.

Day 2: Imitating the humility of Christ

Come unto Me, all you who labour and are overburdened, and I will give you rest.
Shoulder My yoke and learn from Me, for I am gentle and humble in heart.

Mt 11: 28, 29

There is perhaps no single saying in all the Gospels which delineates the character and call of Christ quite as characteristically as this one. Observe: He is conscious of power, conscious of having the power to summon all to Himself for the relief of their ills, their burdens, whether of work or loneliness or neurosis or sickness. He stands forth as the Master and the Compassionate One. And what primarily is He going to do to ease their overburdened hearts? To teach them gentleness and humility that they may be one in spirit and in heart with Him? He did not say 'Learn of Me because I am a loving person'; He demanded primarily that we should learn of Him His gentleness and humility.

These qualities had nothing to do with either timidity or softness of character. He was totally fearless and totally uncompromising. What then was this humility which was so basic to His teaching?

In essence a man is humble when he sees himself as he is in

106

God's eyes; when he perceives his finite size in relation to God's infinity. And this was true even of Christ as man. It did not prevent His extreme intimacy with God His Father, nor hinder the joy and love which flowed through Him; indeed it was basic to this joy and love. For any sort of human pride builds up a wall of self-assertion against the free flow of the divine power within us. There was no such wall in Christ, and the union of the divine and human with Him was such that the human nature accepted the divine with total humility, while the divine Person 'emptied Himself, taking the form of a slave'[1] that He might die a slave's death for the sake of all sinners.

Moreover the life of Christ is set before us by the Evangelists in terms that show us that when God became man He lived in the humblest way from His birth in a manger, through the many years at the carpenter's bench, through the homeless time of His preaching ministry, unto the day of total emptying of Himself on the cross. Quite apart from His teaching, apart even from the consistent welcome He had for the humblest members of society, there was this absolute humility in His own life — a humility which in no way lessened, but on the contrary heightened the authority of His teaching.

And no words can convey the depth of humiliation which He embraced when He yielded Himself out of love for us to the excruciating ignominy of the crucifixion.

Consequently no one commits himself to God with any reality unless he sets himself to learn the virtue of humility in the school of Christ. The first step is to grasp that we are not saved by our own merits, but by pure gift of God. This destroys all foundation for pride.

But pride is a rank weed and contrives to live on all too easily, even when we are aware of its absurdity. Thus it is all too easy for us if we receive spiritual gifts of God to have some feeling of vanity about them. They are *our own* once given, although we never produced them! And the gifts that show the phenomenon of the Spirit working — speaking, prophesying, healing — such gifts can lead to complacency. As has been said already they are not to be confused with holiness, for they are ministerial gifts, given in order that a person may thereby minister in a special way to the Church. But how human we are! Is it not agreeable to be distinguished by such gifts? Does it not give us a certain importance? And contrariwise, am I content if the Holy Spirit has not given me something to manifest? Am I content to be apparently insignificant? In fact no one, no one filled with the Spirit, or who admits the Spirit in full surrender as far as he is able, is ever insignificant or without gifts. For the Spirit has gifts for all.

But it cannot be overstressed that we need to receive all with the most loving humility, and the most humble love. The humility on our side is the most basic quality in our turning to God and our standing before Him, because it is no more than a genuine perception of the truth, and a genuine holding on to it. 'Whence is this to me' cried Elizabeth, 'that I should be honoured with a visit from the Mother of my Lord?' And this she said with a loud cry of joy, when she was filled with the Holy Spirit.'[2]

Those then who feel that the Spirit has worked within them and is still working, and are conscious that He has enriched their souls with mysterious gifts, and delivered them from the sterility of their own poverty, must practise ever increasingly that gentleness and humility of heart which Christ enjoins on them. For this too is part of the harvest of the Spirit within them. Without progress in humility, the crop will prove all too temporary, dry up and wither away. But where there is true humility, the Spirit can answer the yearning of those who desire Him.

Day 3: The spirit of obedience

In the light of the grace I have received I want to urge each one among you not to exaggerate his real importance.

Rom 12: 3

The first consequence of humility of heart is the spirit of obedience. The obedience of the Christian is primarily obedience to God, and to his message; and therefore also to those through whom that message is passed on to us, that is to say those who hold authority in the Church and of whom Christ said: 'He who hears you, hears me; whoever rejects you rejects me',[1] and to whom He said 'Teach them to observe all the commands I gave you.'[2] Thirdly there is the state in which Christians lovingly and joyfully obey one another.

I was once at a charismatic meeting of about thirty persons, including some priests. At one moment, the smallest person present, a child of about ten, asked for some hymn to be sung. Immediately all those present turned the pages of their hymn books to find this hymn, which they then sang; it did not apparently occur to anybody to do otherwise than fulfil this request. This showed that although they were in fact a most varied assortment of people of all ages and walks of life, yet a measure of integration — that 'one heart and soul' of which St Luke speaks[3] — had established itself among them.

It is of great importance that all who are conscious of charismatic gifts and of a lively desire to live more fully in the Spirit, realise that they are not being invited to walk on a path of their own, in some way separated or superior to others who have not yet known their experiences. In every age the Spirit gives His gifts anew in His own way; it seems that in our own He is giving them with great freedom, renewing the vitality of the Church through the manifestation of His power, and the joy of His gifts, and that He reaches out in this to great and small, old and young, learned and simple. But this fresh outpouring is not an abolition or superseding of the accumulated spiritual wisdom and teaching of the Church. On the contrary it will be found to harmonise wonderfully with it. In every age of the Church those whose souls are found to be more advanced in divine ways are always found deeply rooted in humility, and consequently practising a cheerful and ready obedience to those who hold authority over them. The spirit of schism is utterly foreign to those who are filled with the love of Christ's Body.

The more privileged we are, the greater should our spirit of humility be; and we should not take it amiss if at times we feel under-estimated, misunderstood, held in suspicion. This may be very much part of God's plan, so that we may learn to distinguish true humility from false, true resting in God from confidence in ourselves, by the vital test of our not being highly thought of. Here lies the difference between being simply charismatically gifted (wonderful as that may be) and advancing in union with God through the elimination of all that is egoistic in ourselves.

Moreover disobedience or the spirit of disobedience is a sign of pride, of self-assertion, of confidence in one's own judgement; where such a spirit exists it will manifest itself in intolerance. Sooner or later it will prove that the message of the Spirit, though offered, was not understood, and that the gifts of the Spirit, though bestowed, have not been properly used. In the first *Letter to the Corinthians* we get glimpses of this happening, and in other Letters we see the Apostle becoming highly indignant at the failure of some of the members of the Church to keep in line with his instructions or to keep a true grasp of the Christian message and its hierarchy of values. Their failure to understand the need to obey compels him to assert the nature and origin of his apostolic authority. Such tensions can occur. We need therefore to realise always that our commitment to life in the Spirit is a commitment to deeper service of one another, more attentive hearing of the word of God, more complete loyalty to the appointed leaders of the Church.

The point which St Paul makes so gently to the Romans, that each one of them should take care not to exaggerate his own importance, is very relevant to our practice of Christian obedience. For where we take but a modest view of our own importance, gifts, opinions, virtues, we shall find it not too difficult to render due obedience to every one according to their station. Or if we do find it difficult, we shall be alerted to the real nature of the spiritual task ahead of us.

Day 4: Christian love

By this love you have for one another, everyone will know that you are my disciples

Jn 13: 35

The Gospels show us how Christ was ever compassionate in His life and behaviour towards all who come to Him. These were a relatively small number. His invitation and love went out much further, to all of the human race who would pay heed to Him and accept His help. It is, then, a certain sign that we have received His Spirit if we feel ourselves stirred — more than before — to help others. This stirring will not be like ordinary human love in which like cherishes like, nor will it be based on the principle of complementing our personality with some one who fills a gap. These human loves are not to be condemned, but this stirring is something else, a love which is indeed a true love of my neighbour, inspired by the Spirit of God. It is that love, at once universal and individual, which caused Christ to preach the Sermon on the Mount for all mankind, and then to heal the single leper who ran up and knelt before Him;[1] it is the love, inspired by the Spirit which caused Him to stretch out His hands to those sitting in a circle around Him, saying 'Here are my mother and brothers.'[2]

This kind of love for others is the fruit of the Spirit, the first of the list given by St Paul in his *Letter to the Galatians*.[3] We have to translate it into action. It is not something just to be felt, but must prompt always the question 'How can I help this person in need?' Not that we can help everyone, for needs are infinite, but we will become more aware of the needs of those around us, those with whom life brings us into contact; we will feel an urge to do what we can to help where help is needed.

To enable us to fulfil the urge we may receive a gift of helping in some special way. Whether this happens or not, the practice of rendering service to others must become an integral part of our lives, and a constant part also of our prayer lives. For often we have to pray first; this is the first service to render. This will lead us to know what may be done next, unless it is one of those cases in which we have to look to God to provide the solution Himself, and there are many of these.

Thus then, says Christ, are men to recognise his disciples: by their solicitous love for one another. This love is at once a gift from Him and something we have to exercise personally ourselves. By a 'gift from Him' we mean a share of that same loving quality that enabled Him to love all men including sinners, even to the point of dying for them.

This may sound straightforward, a commonplace of religious teaching. But in practice there can be very real difficulty here. Let us say that my life brings me into contact with some one who is harsh, arrogant, tough and ready to inflict pain on me. How can I love that person? Or what of that other person who is petty, mean, deceitful and full of spite? Or so-and-so who has deprived me of my good name or brought my plans to ruin? How can I possibly speak of love for such persons? I have to start by making sure in such cases that I have taken the first step, which is that of forgiveness in the heart. Even so, do they not remain repulsive? The theological distinction between hating the sin but not the sinner is no doubt of great value in the intellectual order, but it will not produce love. Only our Lord can do that, and He may do it by showing how He loves that sinful person, which implies showing something of how He sees them; for very often such persons are themselves victims of others, of an evil system, of a tragic upbringing, of corrupting influences; Christ sees them as victims prostrate under the power of evil and so His redeeming love goes out to them, knowing that there is really quite a different person there in spite of appearances, a person who would both love and desire to be loved, but for the tragic blight which has fallen on him. So Christ continues to love him, seeing always the lovable person He would make him, and indeed probably will make him. We have to learn to share this love and even the vision with Him; but we cannot acquire it ourselves – it remains a gift, a leading example of the harvest of the Spirit.

Love has to express itself both to the individual and the community; otherwise it is incomplete. That means we must seek to be helpful both to individuals and the community in whatever practical ways are available. And if these ways are humble, lowly, inconspicuous, even repulsive to ordinary nature, then let us praise God with joy, for this puts us at the very heart of the working Body of Christ.

Where love is, then there must be the activity of service. And where the Spirit moves there will be love, springing as water from a fountain, silent, crystal clear, refreshing and renewing. So shall men recognise that here is a body of Christ's disciples.

112

Day 5: **The habit of prayer**

Pray all the time, asking for what you need, praying in the Spirit on every possible occasion.

Eph 6: 18

It is through prayer that we practise intimacy with God, and through prayer that we obtain strength to do the things we want to do for Him, and learn the things that He wants us to do for Him; through prayer above all that we render to Him the constant return of our thanks and praise. It is in prayer that we make our petitions, as St Paul indicates, for he goes on '. . . pray for the saints (i.e. fellow Christians), and pray for me . . . pray that in proclaiming (the mystery of the Gospel) I may speak as boldly as I ought to.' The lesson to be grasped here is that, if God on His side adds richness to our prayer, we on our side need to cultivate good prayer habits; and this implies constancy in them.

St Paul indeed supposes that prayer will be a joyful experience. When he says 'pray in the Spirit on all possible occasions,' he includes praying in tongues, in itself a joyful experience, and of value to the speaker,[1] But he does not lose sight of the prayer that is in the Spirit *but is prayed with the mind as well,*[2] prayer that is framed in intelligible language, whether aloud or silent. Liturgical prayer, vocal prayer, silent prayer framed in the mind are all offered with the grace of the Spirit – and St Paul wants the Christian to pray as continuously as possible.

It is a great grace – and one the charismatic may expect – to find prayer a joyful thing. This applies not merely to specific meetings of charismatic groups – but to prayer in general, and not least to the prayer of the Church itself.

But will it always be so? Will not this enthusiasm wane, the fire die down, the embers grow cold? We should learn the lesson which comes from all Christian experience, not to allow ourselves to leave all to the desire of the moment. We need to form and persevere in regular prayer habits whether the Spirit appears to be active at the time of prayer or not. For there will be times when we wonder whether the Other has forgotten the ap-

113

pointment. He has not; but it is very important that we are faithful to the appointment on our side. For we need two things: heavenly joy that we may know how good God is, and hence be drawn to love Him; and the consciousness of our own total poverty, so that we cannot forget that it is not ourselves who produce the fruits, and remain painfully aware that we cannot begin to do so. This is God's way of building a strong foundation for yet greater joy to come, for so we learn to recognise more surely the divine presence when it makes itself felt.

We must then have a timetable, however simple, for prayer, and not leave the matter for God to remind us by a special call each time. Our timetable needs to contain the staple diet by which the Christian nourishes himself; the Sacramental liturgy and some form of vocal prayer such as suits us (many now use the psalms, or the Liturgy of the Hours). This must not be thought of as 'non-charismatic prayer', for in this way too the Spirit prays within us, enlightens and directs our minds and hearts.

It is good to be alert to the needs of those we meet, those we hear of, and of course those we know and live with, who are in need of prayer. Be sure that, when God inspires you with compassion to pray for some one in need, He will answer your prayer[3]. Was not the Saviour inspired by compassion? And will not God answer your prayer if the Saviour teaches you to share His compassion? In this way we may come to have a list of petitions, which after rendering praise and thanksgiving, we bring in full confidence to the Lord. In this world of prayer which we thus enter, God is deaf to no voice, but it is a world in which we have to grow by the exercise of faith and daily communion with the Lord. This caring for others in confident prayer is in itself a proof that the Spirit is at work in us. For His plan of salvation is corporate and calls for our mutual aid, one to another.

Day 6: Healing and prophecy

They will lay their hands on them and they will recover

Mk: 16, 18

I will pour out my Spirit on all mankind; your sons and daughters shall prophecy.

Joel: 2:28 (Acts 2:17)

On Day 2 of Week IV the gifts of healing and prophecy were mentioned briefly. In view of their importance, it may be useful if some additional information is given here.

To be able to heal others is a great gift, and in comparison with the need, few seem to possess it. It was one of the signs by which our Lord said that the preaching of the gospel should be confirmed. He Himself used His divine healing power for that end, but also it seems that He healed men simply because as the Saviour, He was moved with compassion. Is not a Saviour one who saves us from our manifold ills, of which sin is one, but not the only one? And so, moved by compassion, He healed and left a legacy of His powers to His followers.

In fact love in itself is always a healing quality. Much more is it so when love is expanded into divine compassion by the power of the Spirit. To a degree, the healing of the wounds of others is the business of us all. We should pray constantly in this way for others, as our compassion prompts us. If we do this our faith grows deeper, expectancy stronger and we may at last join with others in prayers for healing. Such can be the process by which a healer receives his gift, though it should not be understood that it always comes this way. But always one can say that he cannot claim it for himself, for it is not his power. And he does not always know in advance whether the person desiring healing is to receive the answer through him personally, or that the Lord's plan is different.

Great prudence is necessary in anyone who feels that he is receiving a call to this gift. There is certainly a need for healers and the number is growing. But great purity of heart is needed; total surrender to God's will, even to the point of being willing to look silly, is necessary too. One can respond to the Lord, one can offer oneself, but one must avoid absolutely all self-seeking.

It is worth noting that not all healings are physical; indeed most are what are called 'inner healings' by which the inner wounds and scars of a lifetime are removed; these are psychological and spiritual healings and can occur in conjunction

115

with the Sacrament of Reconciliation. This last is sometimes the background of moral healings or deliverance from sin. For, while the sacrament always brings God's forgiveness for our sins, to be delivered from our bad habits, from the temptation that invariably overwhelms, from the tensions of a losing battle, is not always conceded. It is certainly asked for too rarely.

St Peter [1] quotes *Joel* 2 on the prophets who were to come. Christian prophets were a feature of early Church life. Thus we read: 'While Paul and Barnabas were there (i.e. at Antioch), some prophets came down from Jerusalem, and one of them whose name was Agabus, seized by the Spirit, stood up and predicted that a famine would spread over all the empire.' But the essence of being a prophet did not lie in foretelling the future; it lay in uttering words or admonitions in the person of God Himself. This, then, is a very great gift, of immense aid to the community, though there are the obvious dangers that it may be simulated or used falsely. A prophet has prestige in the community, and anyone who felt an acute need for more prestige might set about prophesying. This is just as true today as it was.

The gift of prophecy has never died out in the Church. Outstanding prophetesses were St Hildegarde (11th Century), St Bridget of Sweden (14th century) and St Catherine of Siena (shortly after St Bridget). But we must not suppose that the gift was confined to big names!

Prophecy is apt to declare itself at charismatic meetings, but often enough with quite small beginnings, as if an electric light bulb glimmered a little for want of a strong current. In such cases the content of the prophecy may not be very striking either. But if the prophet or prophetess is truly called and perseveres courageously, then the stream often grows stronger; it is recognised that God is saying something that nobody else knows how to say, be it rebuke or encouragement or foretelling; such a message receives devout attention.

How shall a true prophet be discerned from a false one, or from some honest person deceiving himself? At first it may not be clear. But normally there are in a community some more experienced members who soon feel uneasy. They make use of the spirit of discernment, and the 'prophet' is asked to subside or even to depart.

Prophecy then like the gift of healing is subject to growth, and can grow from small beginnings to an astonishing capacity to become the mouthpiece of God. Obviously there are dangers, and in general this means that charismatics need to be balanced persons who practise the whole of Christianity; this is certainly not less true of the prophets.

An Archbishop once said to me that he considered that he was the prophet in his diocese. Surely anyone would be rash who denied the prophetic office of the Bishop. As the ruler of the flock the Bishop guides all in God's name. The thoughts and experiences discussed here in no way conflict with these concepts. They deal only with persons whom God touches individually that they may aid specific groups or individuals to serve God more fruitfully. This no more conflicts with the apostolic rights and the gifts that are conferred in the episcopal anointing, than the role of Agabus conflicted with the rights of St Peter and the Apostolic College.

Day 7: Desiring God's gifts

Make love your aim, and earnestly desire the spiritual gifts.
I Cor 14: 1;

In this part of his letter St Paul is clarifying for the Corinthians the nature of the life in the Spirit. Nowhere does he call 'love' a charisma to be classified among the others. The charismata are tools by which love operates. For when we receive the Holy Spirit into our hearts, we receive quite simply God's love – this loving Spirit loves in us, and we make it our aim to correspond. That is why for this love there is no coming to an end, only greater development in time and into eternity. Every stage of our life has to be seen as a stage in which God's love works in us in one way or another: by joy, by trial, by radiance, by darkness – but always that He may give us more. All other qualities or gifts are structured round this central reality of the working of divine love in us. It is at once the goal and the essential feature of the way to the goal, for the Kingdom of Heaven is within us.[1]

The gifts of God referred to above are then to be desired, because they contribute to this progress in the way of God's love. If they are recognised as 'the harvest of the Spirit'[2] then they are the spiritual consequences brought about by this central indwelling love. If they are ministerial gifts for the building up of the Church, such as those listed in Corinthians[3], and elsewhere, they are the tools by which love works. If we recognise in them the effects of the seven gifts of the Spirit of traditional teaching, they are the leading strings of love. St Paul, then, would have us desire all the gifts that God has for us, but let us note that he has already given certain warnings. Spiritual authors have added further warnings, so much so that there could be a danger that we fall into the opposite error – and fail to desire spiritual gifts at all. In fact a lack of expectancy on our part will not help God's plans for us at all. It is He who kindles desire – and then responds to it. We do not escape danger merely by not desiring God's gifts; we fall into the danger of desiring things that are less worthy.

First then, let us desire God's spiritual gifts, but with a sense of our total unworthiness, even with what a medieval mystic calls 'a loving dread'. For fear of the Lord is numbered among the gifts of the Holy Spirit.

Secondly, let us take care that human ambition, the desire to be somebody (Oh, yes, I speak in tongues!) does not enter in. The gifts are for His glory – and if they be ministerial, they are for the sake of others. It is important, then, that our desire should not be egoistic, or motivated with any notion of being important, outstanding, or comparing well with others. In such a case we would almost certainly make a poor use of His gifts and might even give scandal. Our desire must be truly related to our love for God and be a desire to glorify Him more, not that others may glorify us.

Quite apart from comparing ourselves with others, it is possible to err in another way. God gives us a gift; let us say that it is the gift to turn to Him in prayer; or the gift of His protection in some trouble. And we fail to thank Him. We do not notice it, or scarcely. Maybe we are praying for more gifts, higher ones, or things we think more important, and meanwhile He says 'Here is a gift. Take it from me'. And we alas! with our attention turned elsewhere, scarcely take the wrapper off to see and thank Him for what He has already sent us. This failure to take an interest in or be grateful for what He gives us now is an impediment in our relationship with God. For it means that we are more interested in His gifts than in Him, and more interested in 'getting richer' than in His loving kindness to us here and now. This is something to be rejected; it is definitely not what is meant by desiring spiritual gifts. The important thing is that we should have realised that love was the aim.

The Church encourages us to pray for spiritual gifts. She teaches us to pray:

Veni Creator Spiritus! Veni dator munerum!
Come Holy Creative Spirit! Come giver of gifts!

And in one of her most used prayers, she teaches us to pray that 'we may always rejoice in the consolation of the Holy Spirit'. Would we be surprised if He took us at our word? Or do we think that this is a mere state of genial cheerfulness, somehow organised by the Holy Spirit? No, it is His consolation, that is to say the effect of His supernatural gifts, beyond ordinary happiness and ordinary consolation.

This is the whole prayer:

O God who dost fill the hearts of thy faithful with the light of Thy Holy Spirit, grant that we may relish in the same Spirit what is right and just, and always rejoice in His holy consolation, through Christ our Lord. Amen.

Week seven: Now not I

This book does not aim any higher than conveying an elementary knowledge of what the charismatic way is about, and showing that this is in no way destructive of the Church's teaching on baptism, etc. Moreover it is intended as a practical aid — if used as suggested, in conjunction with prayer and towards the receiving a new experience of the working of the Spirit.

The themes treated in the concluding week are:
1. the need for perseverance;
2. thoughts based on the words of St Peter (Day 2) and St Paul (Day 3), warning us not to be overthrown by temptations, trials and sufferings — those accompaniments of Christian life on earth;
3. some final words on developing truly Christian relationships with different sorts of persons, and especially inside the Christian community.

Finally, Day 6 treats of the need for pursuing the reading of Holy Scripture for our ongoing instruction; and also of other aids.

In the last part of our journey we join ourselves with Mary, Mother of Christ, in her song of praise. Catholic tradition has so much experience of the aid that comes from her, that we end the book echoing her prayer, for she is shown, first and last to have been filled with the Spirit of God.

Day 1: Perseverance in commitment

You must give up your old way of life; you must put aside your old self, which gets corrupted by following illusory desires. Your mind must be renewed by a spiritual resolution so that you can put on your new self that has been created in God's way, in the goodness and holiness of truth.

Eph 4: 22-24

Once again this text underlines the call to permanent conversion, and it does not appear to be written (as was the *Letter to the Corinthians*) on account of disorderly behaviour among the converts of Ephesus. But the exhortation to 'give up our old way of life' can come – and does come – appropriately not only to non-Christians, nor only to slack Christians, but also to good living ones, to religious persons. Why? Because God suddenly says 'See, I have more to offer you, far more; will you give more?' The implication is that we examine ourselves, find much of our lives that lies outside the dictation of Christ's love, decide we want to change all that, and to make our lives totally His, not merely by promise, vow, or activity, but in the depths of our heart. Hence we are concerned with the wholeness of our life – that thoughts and desires, ambitions and hopes, leading to words and actions, should all show forth that they are sealed with His love. This is not to be a passing fit of devotion, nor yet the indulgence of spiritually elevating emotions: but a true commitment, the true motivation of our whole life. It is necessary in this last week to renew and deepen this sentiment as much as we may.

For as always there are two sides to the contract. Our side calls for resolution to put some things away, to leave some things behind – and it calls for a certain constancy. We do not find constancy unaided; but we need to realise its necessity, and that God will be with us in its fulfilment. He has to be. For we cannot put away our 'old self' unless there is a 'new self' replacing it, and this 'new self' is the creation of God. We can never create it, nor begin to do so, nor really grasp what it is that God will create. For it will be an individual creation – each person being different, though each will be transfigured by the same Christlike qualities.

What is important is that we do not cling to our 'old self', even in a newly reformed and improved version that we conceive will be our 'new self'. No, our part is to let go, to let Him work His will in us with freedom. The results will be different from our preconceptions, God being a greater artist than we are, and fashioning His creatures with a greater love than we can understand.

Our task then is to remove obstacles to the divine working, to be assured that such obstacles must be there or His love would transform us faster. So our part is active in co-operating with Him, but not exactly creative. The creativity is His. But as Julian of Norwich says 'The continual seeking of the soul pleaseth God full greatly; for it may do no more than seek, suffer, trust', and be ever ready to accept. And if it knows that it has already received much, it must be ready to accept still more.

Here is a text to strengthen you in your resolve and one you can use as a starter for prayer: 'So, my brothers, try even harder to make God's call and His choice of you a *permanent experience*. If you do so you will never fall away'.[1]

Day 2: Temptations and trials

Be calm but vigilant, because your enemy the devil is prowling round like a roaring lion, looking for some one to eat. Stand up to him strong in faith.

I Pet 5: 8, 9

Notice well these words: Be calm, but vigilant. The opposite is to be excited and off one's guard. It is by no means impossible that one who has received a great gift from the Holy Spirit, should get excited and, forgetting some part of the apostolic teaching, be caught, sooner or later, off his guard. This is not because the Holy Spirit lays traps for anyone, nor that the Holy Spirit makes mistakes. But there is one around who does lay traps . . . and catches some victims. Thus, if the Holy Spirit fills us with joy, but we are careless or haphazard in our prayer life, we lay ourselves open to a fall; or if we allow ourselves feelings of superiority, not to say expressions of arrogance, we are already admitting the evil into our system, and allowing that which should be for our purification to be itself corrupted.

Be calm but vigilant. Do not get the idea that nervous tension or a nervous straining in prayer will bring the Holy Spirit or be a sign that He has come. Exactly the opposite. The Spirit brings calm but not somnolence, vigilance (against evil) but not tense nerves. Indeed, where our will is simply yet fully united with the will of our Heavenly Father, this unity which is grounded in a profound faith and is itself the reality of a deep love, cannot but bring calm to the soul; and, since we are one mechanism, this calm will benefit the whole nervous system. Yet this calm is not the enemy of the exuberance of true spiritual joy, for, in the gifts of the Holy Spirit, all good things abound together.

Be vigilant. There will be temptations and trials. By temptations we mean whatever seduces and leads us to prefer other things to God. By trials we mean whatever makes life burdensome, and so attacks our purposefulness, our trust in God, that simple reliance on Him that is so essential to our Christian life. A trial is therefore different from a temptation in this; it can 'lead us into temptation,' it can prepare the way for failure in faith and charity, or contrariwise; if we are vigilant it can serve as a stepping-stone to higher standards of faith and love. That (to repeat a point) is what the *Letter to the Hebrews* is talking about, when it shows how Abraham was repeatedly tested in order that he might be the more abundantly awarded.

It is well to bear in mind that trials often derive their force from our inability to understand them. Why does God allow this to happen to me? Why does He not rescue me? And, most difficult of all is the trial that lies deep in our psychic make-up, such as a state of depression, or permanent state of irritation. . . . The Spirit sometimes heals these things outright in a single moment, and of course this is wonderful! And when He does this, if it is a particularly remarkable case, the story may find its way into print; the recipient of such a favour willingly testifies to the miraculous change in him. But there will be many more cases when the Holy Spirit works more slowly, eliciting an act of faith and trust, a little one; and then responding with what one might call First Aid; and so there arises a process by which little by little He achieves the full effect in the sufferer.

There can be a very good reason for this delayed process. We are intended to be victors in Christ's battle and sing the song of victory with the Lamb,[1] as the *Book of Revelation* portrays. Now a victor has to have a battle. If it is to be his own victory, and so Our Lord wills, he has to join his own small effort to the tidal wave of Christ's victory, and so become one of the vast liberating army which will rejoice for ever in the Kingdom of Heaven. This then can help us to understand the way in which the Holy Spirit gradually fans the flames of faith and hope and love in a person, using also tribulation of some kind as the spur to greater victory.

Trials and tribulations are a normal part of the Christian's life, and Christ undertook his full share of them. But 'by turning everything to good, God co-operates with all those who love Him, with all those He has called according to His purpose.'[2] We have not the key to His design; we see the patch of it in which we are involved as being predominantly of one colour, black or white, grey or gold at a given moment. But lest it should be too hard for us at a time when it appears as an unrelieved black or grey. He leaves at all times the Spirit of God as a pledge in our hearts. Often we may feel this; sometimes He operates strongly without our feeling; always He is there according to the promise:

We can know that we are living in Him,
and He is living in us
because He lets us share His Spirit. [3]

Day 3: Present suffering

For we would like you to realise, brothers, that the things we had to undergo in Asia were more of a burden than we could carry, so that we despaired of coming through alive. . . . It has taught us not to rely on ourselves, but only on God, who raises the dead to life.

II Cor 1: 8

We do not know the details of all that St Paul endured on behalf of the Gospel; but in a very human outbreak (II Cor 11: 23-29) he gives an impressive list of hardships endured such as we should not guess from the *Acts of the Apostles* or from any other letter; we know further that this constant traveller was a sick man, and that he suffered a great deal from the attacks made on him by certain would-be Christians, who undermined his work and tried to destroy his reputation. Nor should we forget that the tribulations still ahead of St Paul at the time he wrote this letter would be no less — for they would include his arrest in Palestine, imminent danger of death, long imprisonment in Palestine, journey as a captive to Rome, imprisonment there . . . finally his death by the sword. It was not then by any means what we should call 'the good life'; far from it.

Hence he has every right to be listened to when he says: 'Yes, the troubles which are soon over, though they weigh very little, train us for the carrying of the weight of eternal glory, which is out of all proportion to them'.[1] This he said from his personal knowledge, for he had been given not only deep insights into the mystery of Christ Jesus, but (if such a distinction can be made) also some experience of the joy to come, and this joy remained with him even as he suffered his trials; this joy he imparted, through the Holy Spirit, to those he converted, and it is against this background of shared joy that he wants them to realise that present suffering does not compare with future joy.

Not that all joy is in the future, for we have 'the pledge of the Spirit'.[2] Now a pledge has a double significance. It is a deposit, a first instalment of a larger sum to be delivered in full later; no man makes a deposit unless he has the intention of going on to complete the contract. The joy, then, that we may receive now from the Spirit is for this purpose – it is God's way of saying to us: 'Here is a first instalment of the whole of your inheritance by virtue of your sonship in me. Is it not good?' And a pledge is also a token, a little something given by one lover to another as a sign of much more. And so God, through the Holy Spirit, creates a certain joy in our hearts that we may grasp that it is the nature of His love to bring us all joy in the fulness of time.

For St Paul, then, our present trials are light-weight in comparison with the weight of glory that is to come, even as our life is a temporary little tent in comparison with that substantial and permanent home which will be ours everlastingly. Yet for us, being ourselves, trials can press very heavily indeed; and even if they do not press so heavily on us, we are likely to know other people on whom they do press. It is important to grasp that suffering is isolating. The sufferer in a hospital bed tends to be isolated with the suffering that is his alone; the sufferer from mental trouble will be even more isolated, agonisingly so. The final journey of death is made alone. But the Holy Spirit working among us can give integration of heart, and therefore power to console. Some people indeed seem to have a power and an aptitude for consoling others; this seems to come from their having happiness to spare, time to spare it, and love to do so. Much more so will this be true when the Holy Spirit unites us and integrates us, so that we do not draw back from the suffering of another with fear or wish to keep his suffering out of sight as do 'the children of this world', but are encouraged by the knowledge that the Spirit of all consolation has visited us, and so, trusting in Him, we have a surety that He will enable us to help others. Thus is the most acute aspect of human trial – its isolating power – overcome.

The Holy Spirit, then, lives in us either not only to strengthen us in our trials, or to carry us through them with joy as He sees fit, but also to enable us to share His strength and His joy with one another in our trials, and thereby to diminish them, as a pledge of their total extinction to come. Indeed, joy is multiplied by the exercise of Christian help. Christians feel that Christ is with them as they feel His joy as they engage in the tasks involved in helping one another and not less so when they are helping non-Christians. For some the power of bringing help, consolation, release from pain or tension may be their especial charism. It is a very lovely one indeed.

Day 4: Behaviour reflects doctrine

It is for you then to preach the behaviour which goes with healthy doctrine.

Tit 2: 1

Towards the end of St Paul's longer Letters he normally leaves doctrinal matters in order to give simple and straightforward counsels on Christian behaviour. The *Letters to Timothy* and to Titus contain a higher proportion of this material. The above brief quotation indicates that there is an essential connection between the two things: a certain type of behaviour evolves inevitably from a loving understanding of true or 'healthy' doctrine. Doctrine which produces peculiar behaviour is not what St Paul calls 'healthy' – and he had experience enough of it. Likewise true Christian behaviour cannot be developed except on the basis of Christian doctrine, understood and accepted according to our personal capacity. For without that understanding we shall be exposed to frustration if we think to be able to carry out the pattern of Christian behaviour.

Hence these brief but pointed instructions at the end of the Letters, addressed to husbands, wives, children, parents, elders, slaves, employers, citizens in their relations to (a very bad) government. . . . Each has his specific Christian contribution to make corresponding to the role which he is playing in the Church, in the family, in society. But one note runs through all the instructions given; it is the note of harmony, of modesty, of lovingness; and corresponding to this is the note of warning against those qualities in us which disrupt harmony. Thus he writes: 'Christ sacrificed Himself for us in order to set us free from all wickedness and to purify a people, so that it could be His very own, and would have no ambition except to do good'.[1] Here he touches the root of so much strife in community – personal ambition, which disguises itself in various ways – desire of rank, desire of influence, conviction that one is right and that one's views must therefore be accepted, a tendency to snipe at others (due really to a feeling that this improves one's own standing), irritation, quarrelsomeness etc.

We must, then, examine ourselves to make sure that we are fulfilling our role in the community in accord with the doctrine that we have received. It will be an altogether healthy sign if we conclude rather ruefully that there is room for improvement; it will not necessarily be the best of signs if we conclude that there is no room for improvement. We should make this examination with respect to our position in the respective groupings to which we belong – family or parish or religious community, or a social unit such as a village or town.

In all our endeavours we need to bear in mind the danger that our aggressive instincts may clothe themselves in high principles, and to make sure that the battles we are called on to fight are truly those of the Lord, and not merely those which we select for the Lord's benefit. For the Christian message is essentially one of harmony and of love one for another; it cannot be propagated successfully by those in whom the love of this harmony has not superseded their personal ambitions or aggressiveness.

The Apostle has a special message concerning our social relations with those who are not believers. Up to a point they apply to social relations generally. 'Be tactful with those who are not Christians, and be sure that you make the best use of your time with them.' This may serve also as a reminder to be tactful with members of another Christian allegiance. But tact is a desirable quality in our dealings with anyone. It is not always found among those who claim to have the Spirit; and yet one would think that the Spirit who adapts himself so sweetly to us – and only uses force when He applies an equivalent amount of restorative – would lead charismatics to an instinctive adaptation to the needs of others. Often this is manifest. But we do well to examine ourselves on this point, realising that tact is not timidity, but a sensitivity to the need of another.

When the Apostle writes 'Be courteous and always polite to all kinds of people'[2] it is not an empty show of courtesy or politeness that he refers to, but an awareness of their needs or their position that is the fruit of true charity and is based on true humility. Humility is the great cure for all arrogance, of which lack of courtesy and politeness are signs.

It can happen that in our mutual relations we may find someone whom we seem destined to come up against, either from natural opposition of view or natural contrast of temperaments or even natural antipathy. In all such cases we should pray earnestly for the other, and frequently. But the object of our prayer should not be that they become converted into our own image and likeness, but that the Father may be fulfilled and glorified in them. How often we have a thing or two to learn ourselves! For example, sometimes people whose characters displease us (not without reason) have got like this through bearing harsh conditions as bravely as they know how. We know that the remedy is love, and that Christ wills to apply His love to them through us.

Day 5: Watching over Christian love

The whole group of believers was united in heart and soul
Acts 4: 32

In these words St Luke records how our Lord's prayer that His followers should be 'One, as we are one', was fulfilled in the early Church. It was indeed with the final words of prayer 'I have made your name known to them, so that the love with which you loved me may be in them, and so that I may be in them,'[1] that He went out to die. Thus the principle of unity among His followers was precisely the recognition of the love that Jesus had for each, and as flame by inevitable attraction joins flame, so the love of Jesus in each drew them together. This is a vastly different kind of unity from that type of common interest or mutual aid which normally draws people together. Nor is it really identical with those efforts which we make to tolerate each other benignly and to get along with our neighbour. Although true charity can well call for such an effort, yet it is not of that which we speak — but of a mysterious uniting love born of a common love in each of us, and such a love as stretches out to comprise all; for it is the love of Jesus Himself, deeper, warmer, more compassionate, more comprehending than our own best efforts.

This love is implanted in us at baptism; it is fed by the Eucharist; it is purified through the Sacrament of Penance. And it is renewed and made more conscious through the grace of the release of the Spirit.

Unfortunately it does seem that the unity of the body — whatever section or fragment of Christ's mystical Body we have in mind — is a fragile thing. It is something which will not be preserved without a high consciousness of its significance and value; and which it will need a true harvest of the Spirit to maintain. Even in the *Acts of the Apostles* we can read of dissension arising almost immediately after Pentecost. 'The Hellenists made a complaint against the Hebrews, that in the daily distribution, their own widows were being overlooked'.[2] This particular matter was quickly settled by the election of seven men as deacons. But the *Acts of the Apostles* tell of other controversies, and the letters of the Apostles, Peter, Paul, John and others bear witness to the fact that in the earliest age there was a struggle for purity of doctrine and that there were rival teachers who had to be resisted and even expelled. Nor does the subsequent story of the Christian Church tell of anything else. Hence we must conclude that this precious gift of unity is to be carefully cherished. In practice this will mean attention at two levels.

Firstly, at the level of doctrine. We have to avoid at all costs doctrinal errors or controversies that will separate us from the teaching and community of the Church. This can never be the path of the Spirit.

To say this does not imply that God has no gifts for those who serve Him in other denominations. God has good gifts for all who serve Him in spirit and in truth, and He loves all His children. We are united to them by these gifts, even if we have to recognise that we are separated by the work of past centuries, through which the seamless robe of Christ was rent. Where such separation has to be recognised, we understand too that the Spirit through His gifts of love and understanding prepares the way for drawing us together again.

Secondly, there is the level of human relationships. We must take the greatest care that no arrogance, no self-assertion, no confidence in ourselves, nor failure in charity to those who disagree with us, impairs the work of the Spirit in the community. This will mean that we must practise self-control to avoid beating down the opinions of others, and humility to repair hurt given. Great as is the aid given to love and charity by the gifts of the Spirit there is always the snare that the very knowledge of privileges received combines in us with personal assertiveness, or ensnares us into thinking less or nothing at all of the opinions of one who is less privileged. In this matter nothing less will suffice than the practice of the fulness of Christ's doctrine[3]:

Blessed are the poor in spirit, for theirs is the Kingdom of Heaven
Blessed are the meek for they shall possess the land; . . .
Blessed are the peacemakers for they shall be called the Sons of God.

Christian unity of heart is a deep and wonderful thing, produced by the Spirit at the deepest level in the hearts of those who are open to receive Him. It is also a fragile thing, easily wounded by our assertive temperaments, sometimes destroyed by them. To preserve it we have need of humility as well as love, and the application of the full range of Christ's teaching, and of the apostolic admonitions.

We can never afford to be off our guard against the appearance in us of the seeds of envy, jealousy, ambition or contentiousness. A good way of being on guard is to give ourselves more fully to the daily service of others as the Spirit shows us.

Day 6: Aids to further development

All Scripture is inspired by God and can profitably be used for teaching, for refuting error, for guiding people's lives, and teaching them to be holy. This is how the man of God becomes fully equipped and ready for any good work.

II Tim 3: 16-17

We have to continue to make progress in our knowledge of spiritual things by frequent reading of Holy Scripture. This may be new for us, or again we may have the advantage of an already extensive knowledge of it. Either way the 'release of the Spirit in us' provides a keener edge to our understanding – the Spirit seems to make His meaning stand out more clearly, more sharply, from the written text, so that we discover that it is inspired indeed. Not all Scripture will necessarily come alive simultaneously; it may do this bit by bit. We have to do our share of the work, but we are conscious of being helped in it.

It is also well to remember that we should not only read Holy Scripture; we should really listen to it when it is read aloud in churches or in the liturgy. For then especially is it being used as it was first intended to be used as a message of God delivered to the Christian assembly for their instruction and guidance. As it is read in the context of the celebration of one of the great mysteries confided to the Church, then it forms one with the Church's prayer – and the two work together for our formation. It would be false to suppose that there is a kind of 'pentecostal spiritual life' to be kept apart from the liturgy and the sacraments. On the contrary, he who is filled with the Holy Spirit will be led to the sacraments with greater expectancy. Particularly is this true of the Mass, and of devotion to our Lord in the Blessed Eucharist. The Liturgy of the Hours now widely used by many people (surely one of the most wonderful reforms to come out of the Vatican Council II) which is largely made up of Scripture, with commentaries by the Fathers of the Church, and additional prayers deeply inspired by the texts, is a natural prayer book for a charismatic and will help him to preserve that objective background which is the characteristic of the Church's prayer. It does not follow that a charismatic will have a lesser appreciation of whatever devotions he followed before – that may well depend on what those devotions were – but through a growing love of scripture he will find that the Church's own Liturgy of the Hours is a source of growing attraction.

Scripture is not the only source from which 'the man of God becomes fully equipped and ready for any good work'. Today there are available many spiritual and theological works in which the latest insights into our faith are expounded. Indeed if anything the problem is that they are so many, and so diverse as to cause bewilderment. A ceaseless stream of literature represents a very lively period in the history of the Church, but not all of it is equally valuable nor equally sound. We will do well not to give ourselves indigestion. It is advisable to read with a view to getting a good grasp of the doctrines of our faith, or if we have that already, to bring our knowledge into line with the progress in the Church. St Ignatius Loyola is responsible for the advice 'sentire cum Ecclesia', to share the mind of the Church, and this implies learning her mind. Particularly will this be necessary when the Church reviews her sacraments, and decides that she has new things to say about them.

What may be called classical spiritual works should not be thought of as out of date. They have their own degree of inspiration. This is at a great distance indeed from that of Holy Scripture and not of the same quality, for they do not add to or contain revelation. But they are inspired in the sense that the warmth of the love of the servant of God and his or her profound insight into the ways of God penetrate their pages and give them a permanent value that speaks across the ages to lovers of God at all times. It is good, then, if we have time and disposition, to read them; yet it is well to bear in mind that they are inevitably conditioned by the culture of the time and country which gave them birth; hence an introduction by a specialist illustrating their specific qualities and why they emphasise certain matters or do not emphasise others, is of value; for they were not written in a cultural vacuum. Their witness to the wonderful work of God in the souls of the writers is of permanent value, but needs to be understood in its own context. The choice is vast, so that we do well to read what helps us, rather than to aim at quantity. It is better to read a little with profit, than to read over much.

Reading, then, Holy Scripture in the first place, and other works according to our possibilities and circumstances, will be one of the means through which the Holy Spirit communicates Himself in fresh lights to our souls. It should be a part of our lives.

Day 7: Mary's Prayer

And Mary said: 'My soul proclaims the greatness of the Lord, and my spirit exults in God my Saviour. Because He has looked upon His lowly handmaid.'

Lk 1: 46

St Luke has already shown us Mary at the moment of the great announcement made to her on behalf of the whole human race. He has made clear the message: 'The Holy Spirit will come upon you and the power of the Most High will cover you with its shadow.'[7] Now we are given the prayer that comes spontaneously from her heart. It is a prayer that illustrates the thoughts and inspirations of the spirit-filled soul.

My soul proclaims the greatness of the Lord. The song of praise lies at the beginning of true prayer. Our Lord taught us this Himself. When you pray, He said, you shall say: 'Father in heaven, may your name be held holy.'[1] The first thing is the praise of God because it is His due, because it is right and just, because it acknowledges also our debt to Him. It is the constant refrain of the Psalms, which are essentially hymns of praise. It is natural that the spirit-filled soul of Mary should break out first of all into the praise of God. Charismatics observe that, in general, where in a meeting the praise of God abounds, so also do gifts abound.

My spirit exults in God my Saviour. The next note is of joy. The

135

Greek word translated here as 'exults' means literally 'to rejoice with exceeding great joy', or, more colloquially 'to jump for joy'. It is joy of the Spirit which fills her. There are those who, from a long tradition, will react with suspicion and distrust to signs of joy occurring at times of common prayer. They have settled for prayer that is totally controlled and disciplined and orderly. These are excellent qualities, but spiritual joy, too, must be allowed to express itself. For Mary, praise of God is swiftly followed by exultation in the Spirit.

He has looked upon his lowly handmaid. Swift on the heels of joy comes the expression of her lowliness of condition. Everyone in whom the Spirit works is bound to acknowledge the lowliness of their condition, the utter gratuitousness of God's favours to them. And for us, unlike Our Lady, there is the conciousness of sin, making us so much the more unworthy of the divine gift.

These three notes, praise, joy and humility, are the opening strains of Mary's song.

Yes, from this day forward all generations shall call me blessed. So Mary enters the ranks of the prophetesses. Not inaptly the Litany of Loreto calls her the Queen of Prophets.

For the Almighty has done great things for me, and holy is His name. It is a notable characteristic of the Christian saints that they show an unwillingness to reveal the great things that God has done in them; this is because they want neither the praises nor the curiosity of the world. So this humility causes them to seal up God's gifts to themselves. But sometimes, as with Mary, God so fills them with joy, exultation and praise at what He has done, that they are compelled to bear witness to the great goodness of God shown in these workings, and to cry aloud: Holy is His name. It is an overpowering need to testify to God's wonderful love for us.

The next themes are God's mercy, and his protection, to those that fear Him, those that serve him with reverential fear of the Lord (cf Isaiah 11, 2-3, Week IV, Day 5) and His power to deal with His enemies. There is a contrast too between God's satisfying those who are hungry, and His dismissal of those who are already satisfied. The hungry, who are they but ourselves? We who sense deep desires, beyond human fulfilling, and who turn to Him in our hunger and our thirst. The well-filled are those who are satisfied with the comforts and pleasures of the world, and who do not know the divine dissatisfaction that turns them to God. Of these it is written: 'Alas for you who have your fill now; you shall go hungry.'[2] And what of those who, although not absorbed in worldly things, have no hunger for the gift of the Spirit, but are content as they are, and prefer not to be invaded by Him? 'You say to yourself; I am rich . . . and have everything I want, never realising that you are wretchedly and pitiably poor.'[3]

He has come to the help of Israel his servant, mindful of His mercy. So concluded Mary's prayer. The ultimate basis of our total confidence is always that God is never forgetful of His promises, is ever mindful of His promise of mercy. Thus we confidently address our prayers to the Lord, not on the strength of our merits, but rather because our emptiness, our hunger, our thirst, make their claim on Him who alone can enrich us with the kind of good things we really need.

The fiftieth day

Then a voice came from the throne; it said: Praise our God you ser-
vants of His, and all who, great or small, revere Him. And I seemed to
hear the voices of a huge crowd like the sound of the ocean or the roar
of thunder, answering: 'Alleluia! The reign of the Lord our God
Almighty has begun; let us be glad and joyful and give praise to God,
because this is the time of the marriage feast of the Lamb. His Bride is
ready, and she has been able to dress herself in dazzling white linen,
because her linen is made of the good deeds of the saints.

Rev 19: 5-8

Let us end these pages with the thought of this heavenly voice
that bids us 'praise our God' and evokes the thunderous sound of
victory that issues from the throats of the multitudes who thank
Him for their everlasting salvation. Let us – from among His
many good gifts – thank Him particularly for three things: for
the gift of our creation, our being called out of nothing, which is
the basis on which He will build all subsequent joy; for the gift
of our Redemption or buying back, through the sequence of His
Incarnation, His bitter Passion and Death and His triumphant
Resurrection; and thirdly for the gift by which He calls us now,
at this moment to respond to Him, to turn to Him with trust and
surrender.

Let us bear in mind that we progress surely, in God's hands,
towards this heavenly court of great and small blessed ones, and
that the reign of the Lord our God Almighty has already begun
in us. We have but to go forward in confidence, knowing with
certainty that His goodness will not slacken or diminish or lack
power; on the contrary, we as yet grasp little of the joy that is to

139

come when the barriers between us and God are finally down, and we attain the fulness of the marriage feast of the Lamb of God. Meanwhile the voice bids us to be glad and joyful; incessantly to thank and praise God.

It is indeed of our human nature that we cling to our life here and turn fearfully away from whatever threatens it. We feel as St Paul puts it, that we do 'not want to strip it off, but to put the second garment (i. e. eternal life) over it, and to have what must die taken up into life. This is the purpose for which God made us'.[1] Life being the purpose for which God made us we cannot forget it for a moment, and accept with difficulty the prospect of any sort of dissolution of it. Hence God's answer to our problem is that we shall have the joy of the hereafter brought forward into the now. So that in effect the stripping off of our present garment, the termination of our life on earth, shall not appear to us, nor affect us as that end and termination which we so dread. And for this end God 'has given us the pledge of the Spirit'[2] in our hearts, to give us a foretaste of the joy of the hereafter now, and to enable us to feel that confidence through which we make the total surrender which eliminates fear. This pledge may make itself felt softly in faith, strongly in love, surprisingly in joy. But it will remain always with us. For God's word is sure, and we do Him grievous wrong if we give Him less than total trust in His loving care.

This pledge of the Spirit within us is what impels us to say to Him with the psalmist: 'My heart has said of you: seek his face'.[3] For now it knows no division of purpose, but goes out to Him in full acceptance, knowing that it is accepting the divine invitation to share everlastingly in God's glory.

Meanwhile it is for each of us to make his contribution by good works to the fulness of Christ's Kingdom here on earth, so that his Bride may be able to dress herself in dazzling white linen, because her linen is made of the good works of the Saints. So we make our contribution day by day, hour by hour, and through the works and prayers that grace prompts us to do, we are prepared for fuller glory when He sees that the time is come.

'And he said to me: Write this: Happy are those who are invited to the wedding feast of the Lamb.'[4]

Let us write it on our hearts.

140

To Him who, by means of the power working in us is able to do so much more than we can ever ask for, or even think of: to God be the glory in the Church and in Christ Jesus, for all time and for ever and ever! Amen.

Eph 3: 20-21 (trans. Good News for Modern Man)

Notes and References

Week One
Day 2 1. Acts 1: 7, 8
       2. Acts 5: 42
       3. Jer 31: 34
       4. Is 55: 9
Day 5 1. Heb 2: 10
       2. Heb 2: 14
       3. Rom 5: 7
       4. Mk 15: 39
Day 6 1. Is 53: 4-6
       2. Jn 15: 13
       3. Heb 5: 8
Day 7 1. Mt 21: 18

Week Two
Day 3 1. Mk 15: 39
       2. Jer 31: 34
Day 4 1. Jn 10: 11
Day 5 1. Jn 7: 37, 38
       2. Is: 55, 1
Day 7 1. Mt 6: 6
       2. Mt 18: 20

Week Three
Day 1 1. Ezek 36: 26
       2. Jn 10: 10

Day 2 1. Jn 17: 4
2. Lk 12: 49, 50
3. Mt 13: 23; Jn 75: 5
4. Heb 4: 16
5. Heb 2: 3, 4

Day 3 1. I Cor 12: 3
2. Gal 4: 6

Day 4 1. Following the note in the *Jerusalem Bible*
2. Jn 14: 16
3. Acts 1: 4-5
4. Acts 2: 36-39

Day 5 1. Acts 10: 47, 48
2. Acts 8: 14-17
3. Acts 19: 5-6
4. I Cor 3: 2

Day 6 1. A more complete and precise definition is given by Father Francis Sullivan SJ. He defines baptism in the spirit as a religious experience which initiates a decisively new sense of the powerful presence and working of God in one's life, which working usually involves one or more charismatic gifts.
2. Jn 3: 8

Day 7 1. Acts 8: 18, 19
2. A much fuller list of the effects to be expected after receiving the baptism of the Spirit is to be found in *The Life of the Spirit Seminars:* Team Manual, pp 119-121. Our text refers only to such as lie inside the limited scope of this book, and are widely experienced.

Week Four
Day 1 1. Mk 4: 26
2. Mt 7: 16

Day 2 1. I Cor 12: 27-29, Eph 4: 11-12, Rom 12: 6-8
2. Rom 12: 6-8
3. Heb 6: 4-5
4. Stephen Clark: *Spiritual Gifts.* Another study is by Arnold Bitlinger: *Gifts and Graces*

5. Mt 7: 15
6. I Cor 14: 39
Day 3 1. I Cor 12: 30
2. I Cor 14: 23
3. I Cor 14: 18
4. I Cor 14: 7
5. Rom 8: 26, 27
6. I Cor 1: 7
7. I Cor 12: 1
8. Cf. 1 Thess 5: 19; I Cor: 14, 40
Day 4 1. Acts 2: 39
2. Acts 3: 1-10
3. Acts 4: 21
Day 7 1. Lk 1: 47-47

Week Five
Day 1 1. Mt 9: 17
2. cf Heb 3: 7 'Today as the Holy Spirit says, today . . .'
(NEB) which in its turn comes from Ps 94: 7
3. *Life* (by herself): 31: 24
4. I Cor 1: 4, 5
Day 2 1. I Cor 6: 9
2. Ps 18: 29
3. ibid 32
Day 3 1. Is 53: 3
2. Mt 11: 28
3. Gal 5: 22
4. Mk 2: 5
Day 4 1. Qoh 7: 10
2. Mt 6: 14
3. Mt 18: 23-35
Day 7 1. Ps 23 (Authorised Version)

Week Six
Intro 1 1. Ph 3: 14 (NEB)
Day 1 1. Lk 9: 23
2. Mt 10: 38

3. Mt 5: 10
4. 1 Chron 29: 10 (Vulg)

Day 2 1. Ph 2: 7
2. Lk 1: 41, 42

Day 3 1. Lk 10: 16
2. Mt 28: 20,
3. Acts 4: 32

Day 4 1. Mt 8: 1, 2
2. Mt 12: 50, Mk 3: 34
3. Gal 5: 22

Day 5 1. I Cor 14: 4. The NEB translates: 'The language of ecstasy is good for the speaker himself' – but ecstasy normally implies that the speaker is in some sense outside himself or deprived of self-control. This is not so (except occasionally at the beginning) with the gift of tongues.
2. I Cor 14: 15
3. cf. Dame Julian of Norwich, to whom our Lord said: 'I am the Ground of thy beseeching; first it is my will that thou have it; and after I will make thee to will it, and since I make thee to beseech it, and thou beseechest it, how should it be then, that thou shouldst not receive thy beseeching?' And she explains: 'Beseeching is a new, gracious lasting will of the soul, oned (united) and fastened into the will of our Lord by the sweet inward work of the Holy Ghost'. *Revelations,* ch 41.

Day 6 1. Acts 2: 17
2. Acts 11: 27–28

Week Seven
Day 1 1. 2 Peter 1: 10 (NEB)

Day 2 1. Rev 15: 3-4
2. Ròm 8: 28
3. I Jn 4: 13

Day 3 1. II Cor 4: 17
2. II Cor 5: 5

Day 4 1. Tit 2: 14
2. Tit 3: 2

Day 5 1. Jn 17: 26
2. Acts 6: 1

 3. Mt 5: 3, 4, 9
Day 6 1. Mk 1, 41
Day 7 1. Lk 1: 35
 2. Lk 6: 25
 3. Rev 3: 17,

The Fiftieth Day
1. II Cor 5: 4, 5
2. ibid
3. Ps 27: 8
4. Rev 19, 9

Also published by
Darton, Longman and Todd

DID YOU RECEIVE THE SPIRIT?
By Simon Tugwell OP
YOU HE MADE ALIVE
By Peter Hocken
NEW HEAVEN? NEW EARTH?
By Peter Hocken, Simon Tugwell OP, John Orme Mills OP
and George Every
A NEW PENTECOST?
By Léon-Joseph, Cardinal Suenens
WAYS OF THE SPIRIT
By Léon-Joseph, Cardinal Suenens (edited by Elizabeth
Hamilton)
COME HOLY SPIRIT
By Léon-Joseph, Cardinal Suenens and Archbishop Michael
Ramsey